Hunting the Sun

Hunting the Sun

A Passion for Grouse

by

Ted Nelson Lundrigan

Foreword by
Michael McIntosh

Illustrations by
Steven C. Daiber

COUNTRYSPORT PRESS
Traverse City, Michigan

This edition of *Hunting the Sun* was designed by
Angela Saxon of Saxon Design, Traverse City, Michigan.
The text is set in Goudy.

First edition
10 9 8 7 6 5 4 3 2 1

Published by Countrysport Press
1515 Cass Street, P.O. Box 1856
Traverse City, Michigan 49684

Printed in the United States of America

Library of Congress Cataloging-in-Publication Data

Lundrigan, Ted Nelson.
   Hunting the sun : a passion for grouse / by Ted Nelson Lundrigan :
foreword by Michael McIntosh ; illustrations by Steven C. Daiber. --
1st ed.
        p.   cm
   ISBN 0-924357-70-3
   1. Ruffed grouse shooting--Minnesota--Anecdotes. 2. Lundrigan,
Ted Nelson. I. Title.
SK325.G7L85   1997
799.2'4635'09776--dc21   97-21759

Contents

Foreword vii

1   The Second Cutting 1

2   The Watch 7

3   Middle Sea 17

4   The Cartway of Time 27

5   The Bridge Bird 35

6   Sporting Goods, Row Three 45

7   Turner's Windrow 57

8   Whose Woods These Are 69

9   A Slide Inclination 81

10 Remember Me This Way 93

11 The Magic Gun 109

12 One Good Turn 125

13 Bookends 141

14 More 153

15 Birds in Seisin 165

16 In Green Pastures 177

17 In the Public Domain 193

18 The Wagon Wheel............................ 203

19 A Square Mile 215

20 Packing for the Trip 227

Foreword

Soon after this first appears in print, frosty nights and a chill north wind will be sending bright-gold aspen leaves tumbling through the Minnesota woods like flung coins, and I'll be there to see them for the eighteenth season of hunting grouse with Ted Lundrigan.

Not, unfortunately, for the whole season, because I live a long way from there, but certainly for as many days as I can wring from what I do for work and he from his law practice. It's that way every year, and after seventeen seasons those days have tallied up quite a few. Some careers, jail terms, and marriages don't last as long.

My love affair with northern Minnesota and my friendship with Ted started at the same time. I was less than two months short of my thirty-fifth birthday. Ted was a couple of years younger than I and the countryside a lot older. Now

I'm looking at fifty-two. Ted's still a couple of years younger, and the countryside is still a lot older.

It and I show a bit more signs of age than he does. His mustache is turning a bit silvery, but he's just as able to walk me into the ground, and just as kind about giving me the easier going when my knees start to give out. Some things don't change.

Other things do. Some of the coverts we hunted for years are now inaccessible or too mature to hold birds or just plain gone. Places like Covey Top and Bee Sting, Disco and Byron's Demise, Sam's Rest, Mike's Revenge, and Ra-a-a-y Charles are huntable now only in memory, replaced by newer, younger coverts like Cow Trails and Ghillie Pasture and some others.

Even so, thanks to timber management, the vagaries of chance, or just pure good fortune, some of the places he showed me the first day we spent together are as huntable now as ever. Just last season we moved birds on the Green Trail, at the Tractor Site, the Cookie Jar, in Turner's Windrow, the Wagon Wheel, the Bridge covert, and more.

These, and places like them, are the central threads that weave the texture of this book—for at its best, grouse hunting is about places and time, about the land and the lessons it teaches as we learn to recognize the difference between what changes and what doesn't.

I imagine it's not particularly unusual for one man to spend a lifetime hunting just a few square miles of cover. But make him a thoughtful, introspective man who seeks to discover meaning in what he does, school him in the craft of language, and give him leave to combine them all—and something special is likely to come of it. Something of rare worth and beauty. Something like this book.

It is not without precedent, through more than one descent of lineage. Burton Spiller hunted the same New England coverts much of his life and wrote what now stands as the classic body of grouse-hunting literature. Dana Lamb and John Alden

Knight were grouse hunters, attorneys, and skillful writers, and they, too, contributed to the classical canon. Ted Lundrigan is all of those things, and the book he has written is exactly the book I knew he'd write if he ever succumbed to my urging to write a book on grouse hunting.

I don't suppose we'd exchanged more than two or three letters in the year after we first hunted together before I knew there was a writer with something important to say waiting in the wings. Simply put, the lad can spin a tale with the best.

His wit is sometimes dry, sometimes as piercing as a hot needle, but either way, he can be funny, and being truly funny is an extremely difficult thing to do in writing. Unlike most of what passes for humor in this field, his comic passages are neither bitter nor merely silly. If you don't laugh out loud a dozen times before you finish this, you don't have a funny bone.

He can also drop a bait that lands as gently as a #20 dry fly and have you in the net before you realize you've been had. I'll let you find those for yourself, but he once nailed me dead-center writing about finding an overgrown cemetery way back in the woods beyond a covert he knew I'd recognize (and therefore believe). He made it as real as if I was there with him, pulling brush and snarls of grass away from the weathered headstones and uncovering one whose nearly-gone chiseling read "Here lies somebodyorother, a fine attorney and an honest man."

I never even felt the hook till I got to the last sentence, which read, "You know, it's not very often you find where they put two guys in the same grave."

Most of all, though, Ted can touch your heart, no matter whether he's talking about the land or the birds or the dogs or just making you realize that hunting grouse and living are all the same thing. If you don't go back and read "The Bridge Bird" and "Packing for the Trip" at least twice, I'll buy the drinks.

It's mightily tempting to keep on with this, to tell you about old Dixie and Salty and Bill and Spence and all the rest. I was there when a lot of this happened. But this is not my book, though I can honestly say it's one I truly wish I'd written. Better you should hear it from Ted. That way, you'll get to know him, too, and understand that he's the kind of hunter—and the kind of man—John Madson had in mind when he wrote his lovely little poem, "The Pa'tridge Hunter":

> *None breathes Autumn more deeply than he*
> *and none makes better use of bright October.*

And none, I might add, makes better use of blank sheets of paper.

—Michael McIntosh

To the mirror of my soul:
Hunting partners past, present,
human and canine

The earth don't want to just keep things, hoard them;
it wants to use them again. Look at the seeds, the acorns,
at what happens even to carrion when you try to bury it:
it refuses too, seethes and struggles too until it reaches
light and air again, hunting the sun...
—William Faulkner
Big Woods

We, compounded of dust
And the light of a star.
—Loren Eiseley

Language best shows the man,
Speak that I may see thee.
—Ben Jonson

Chapter 1
The Second Cutting

A man climbed a tree at the edge of the central Minnesota prairie, so the story goes, and looked to the north. He saw the vast pine forest and declared that it would take ten thousand men one thousand years to cut down all the trees. He was wrong. By the early 1900s it was pretty much gone. The ax and the two-man saw had converted the great pine forest into lumber to build America. The timber companies transferred the stump-covered sand hills to their land companies, which in turn sold them to the Norwegians, Finns, and Germans whose money could not afford the good black land to the south and west. It was these northern Europeans, used to poor land and hard winters, who stepped off the train in my small village and headed west into the maple hills.

The basement holes that I find in the corners of old pastures prove that cement was expensive and rocks were plentiful. Old walls that now hold the cans, bottles, and scrap steel of two or three hard-scrabble farmers show me that most of the pilgrims were gone by the end of the 1930s. The depression did them in. It wasn't a dust-bowl drought that withered their resolve, but the fact that whatever they could produce from these hills had little value. They probably never ate better. Cattle were hauled from the parched south and left free to roam the creeks and valleys. The grouse prospered as the poplar spread and were so easy to gather that a farm boy was expected to kill a few when he brought the cows in. Everything had a price, but the wealth that was so easily available to the farm—the crops, the meat, the wild game—had no cash value. Then, as now, it was money that was needed.

The outbreak of World War II pulled the people from the maple hills and into the city. There they could find the cash that was so scarce in the woods. Behind them they left the old pastures, cow yards, and weedy fields. The trails from one neighbor to the next, across the low-water fords and over wood bridges, grew into clover and grass. The poplar trees grew high and the field edges became thick with berries. The hills became tall once again. Thousands of acres forfeited back to the state for unpaid taxes. Land was plentiful and the ruffed grouse, ever the opportunist, filled in the gaps.

When I was a boy I could—and did—walk through the village with my shotgun uncased. My friend Donny and I liked to shoot the crows that gathered around the dump. He lived on the outskirts of town and I would walk to his house carrying a long and heavy Remington Model 29 pump shotgun under my arm. I had enough sense not to ride my bike and try to manage the gun at the same time. It was unloaded. But given my size, and the length of the gun, there could not have been any mistaking it for a golf club or ball bat. Today I'd be stopped by seven or eight camouflage-clad deputies and carried off to juvenile court to explain to a puzzled magistrate how I could have had such a profound lapse of judgment. But then (and we are talking about the early 1960s) a friendly wave to a yard-working neighbor was all that was necessary for safe passage.

My point is that times change. I live in the same town, and even though I am the city attorney and a person of some influence and respect from my years of country lawyering, I

suspect that those seven or eight camo-clad deputies would be in my face, asking for the immediate possession of the shotgun. And my Westley Richards 20-gauge is a lot smaller and more inconspicuous.

There is an illustration on page 33 of William Harnden Foster's book, *New England Grouse Shooting*. A lanky eastern farmer is leaving the dooryard of his homestead with his bird dog leaping about his feet. His double gun is in the crook of his left arm and he is turning his head to speak over the other shoulder to a pleasant-looking woman standing in the doorway. It is going to be a long walk. Foster writes that in those days before the hard road and the automobile, such a man had his own "covers" and most of the gunning was done on foot from home. A hard-walking man with a good dog could melt into the country, and by knowing where to cross and how to connect the locations he would reappear at sundown with a tired dog and a full game bag.

I have such a place.

My heart, at least that part of it not given to my wife and children, is in those hills and centered on that place. Nowadays I drive my old hunting car on hard roads, then gravel, and finally onto a grass-centered trail, where I bump and wade my way to the final climb, avoid the washout on the right, and turn into the driveway. The three-wire suspension between the posts passes for a gate, and with a knowledge gained by practice it is opened, then closed behind me. I have permission to be here.

If all the world could watch it would see the same ritual every time. After the gate is hooked I walk up to my car rubbing my hands, one over the other, in the universal wordless human gesture that says, "Oh boy!"

My bird dogs, free to roam the soiled interior, issue a vocal second, and together we growl along in low gear, crowding the earth side of the road cut into the hill until the little house comes into view around the corner. It is here that I can see the lanky bird hunter of Foster's drawing with his eager dog and the quiet woman at the open door. It is from here that a hard-walking bird hunter can connect wonderful places together and return with tired feet and worn-out dogs, and, most of the time, a game bag stuffed with memories.

Every place that I hunt is within ten miles of here. There are roads—some tar, some gravel—and trails that divide this land into the grid that civilization requires for possession. But when these sturdy Scandinavians broke the earth there was only one road. I have found its tracks here and there. Sometimes it is traced into a side hill like the one just traveled, and in another place it is a crossing at the streamside with just the slightest elevation leading down to it. The cement walls of a grand old house mark the passage in another place, and I found the remains of a horse-drawn gravel scoop lying in an eroded cut over that hill to the south.

If I lived in this small square house I could walk this trail and leave it from time to time to hunt a clump of dogwoods in one place, or a poplar thicket in another, but I can't live here. I, too, need to make money. To do that in the best and most efficient way I have to be in another home. That is the reality of life and economy. Bird hunters are travelers. Most think nothing of the several hundred miles that separate them from where they work and where they want to be. They will have no financial gain for covering such a distance, and the biggest grouse in the world is still smaller than a supermarket chicken. So it is the place that matters in the final analysis.

Grouse have been hunted out East, in the grand tradition of the apple orchards and stone walls, for two hundred years. Here in Minnesota the tradition is more recent. A hundred years ago, before the bird hunter, there were only the great long-needled pines. These went down under the cutter's edge. Then the settler came and pushed back the remains of the forest to try to make the sand produce life for his crops. But the poplar and the grouse were patient and omnipresent, and when all but the most tenacious farmers left, they filled in whatever was empty.

Now the poplar has value. This second cut promises to be larger than the first. The face of the land will be changed by the great machines that cut and haul the trees. There is good news: the farming will be no better here than it once was, and the poplar will be encouraged to return to the new open places.

Before this happens you and I will leave this small house along the old trail. In the following chapters I will share with you what I learned in this center of my world. Because when the poplar comes up again I will be somewhat older and it is possible that my feet won't pick themselves up like they used to.

Chapter 2
The Watch

The water had run out of the farm pond, finding its way, like a pet turtle. When the muddy latticework of the old beaver dam had crumbled in the drought, the sluice keepers had apparently moved on downstream. It was so dry that the leaves shattered when the bird shot struck them, leaving a halo of suspended dust and debris.

A grouse had been right in the center of that cloud. I hunted with my Labrador retriever Dixie in those early years and she had flushed this bird to my right. It crossed low in the understory, diving to reach the bottoms of Wood Row Creek. She stood at my feet, panting for a drink, looking with her perpetual worried expression toward the dribble of water that would be out in the tall yellow grass.

We had come a long way, farther than ever before. I pulled my bandanna from my hip pocket, took the wire-rim glasses from my face, and wiped the lenses clean. Weaving them back over my ears, I turned toward the streambank.

"Let's go, girl," I said. "We'll look for the bird or water; either one will be as good as the other."

It was a short push through the brush to clear the woods. She trotted past me, skidded down the earth bank, and disappeared into the yellow valley. In a moment I could hear a steady lapping followed by a contented splash as she lay down in the cool mud.

"I wish I could do that, too," I mumbled, and looked for a place to rest.

On the far side, across the creek bottom, was a clump of tall Norway pines, and on the edge of it the visible corner of a wood-shingled house roof. Tall stumps were scattered throughout the grassy sea, each one flat-topped at about hip height. I walked over to the nearest one and examined it. Now that the water was gone it was easy to get up close. This one and the others around it were oak, or possibly ash. They had been cut off by a two-man saw, which was why they were all so tall and uniform. The roots of the nearest was washed clean of earth and bark and formed a comfortable bowl for a chair and a gun rest. I slid the action open and rested the little pumpgun securely in a notch, settling down next to it.

This place had not felt the sun for many years. "Probably not since the depression," I said aloud. My pipe was in the bottom of my left vest pocket along with a tobacco pouch, matches, safety pins, dirt, leaves, and two empty shell casings.

"One of the great benefits of pipe smoking," I continued, "is that it gives the puzzled hunter something to do while he figures out where he is at." I packed the bowl methodically and eyed the far roof corner. Soon a great cloud of fragrant smoke floated across the grass tops, drifting over the hidden mud wallow and my happy dog. Now we were both content.

I wasn't lost. You have to care where you're at to be lost. Besides, that was an old hay field just to the left of the roof and it carried down to this stream. *So, this is the far edge of the old Pedersen place.* The long dry summer had given me passage across the swamp where, in other years, I had turned back to keep my feet dry. I had followed the flush of three grouse through a long cluster of gray dogwood bushes, taking one and missing the last. I was sure now that I had missed. *The pattern was tearing through bushes just a few yards away,* I reasoned. *If it was in the center then, the shot was behind when it got to where he was at.*

Well reasoned, I complimented myself, and patted the soft lump in my game bag. I leaned back against the bare trunk of the stump and stared up at the cloudless September afternoon. Next to my left shoulder the wood was split where a part of the tree had broken off before the rest was cut. It formed a bowl of sorts, surrounding the core with a sheltering cover a foot or so above the high-water mark.

In the middle there was the soft wood of the rotted center, some nutshells, and something else. The bowed edge of a metal object, soft gold, with an engraved line.

I tugged the glove off my right hand, stuffing it between the buttons of my old cotton shirt. Then with my fingers I dug carefully at the accumulation of bark, debris, and dry wood. Finally I could grasp the object with my thumb and forefinger, and I lifted it out of its packing.

It was a gold pocket watch.

I leaned back against the stump and held it in the sun. I turned it one way, then another, rubbing the surface clean with my thumb.

"Howard" was printed on the clock face under a slender minute hand pointed at twelve. An hour hand of glistening blue steel indicated the number eleven. Underneath was a small numbered face and a sweep second hand. On the back was the engraving that I had first seen: "E.H.C.," it read.

Hearing heavy breathing, I looked up into the quizzical eyes of Dixie, my retriever. "I found a watch, see?" She snuffed it, then lay down with a groan and went to sleep. "That is your problem; you have no sense of curiosity."

The watch had been there for many years. Apparently it had been placed on the stump by its owner or had fallen or been nudged into the narrow slit between the trunk and the broken limb. Here was the mark of another man who had spent the day following his nose. The watch stared sightless up at me. It wasn't a bad symbol of that wandering, but whose was it?

I tamped another load of tobacco into my pipe and thought of the town not too far from here, and of the farm across the stream.

This was not a farmer's watch; this was the possession of a man with money as well as time. Those hard-rock farmers across the little valley had felled these trees, hauled the logs out of here, cut them into lumber, and built the barn first, then the house. They had no money for ornaments. They would not have bought a gold watch when silver-plated tin would tell time as well. No, this belonged to a town sportsman. Someone who, like myself, parked his car or buggy where Wood Row Creek crossed under the township road, and then worked his way upstream to this place. He may have been a trout fisherman, for there were trout here before the beaver warmed the water, or he may have been a bird hunter. Either way this was his secret place, because both kinds guard their success closely.

I looked around and tried to imagine another time when the stream was running fast and cold and the trees were fresh cut. There must have been alders here and new dense growth in the area just below the old beaver dam. The line of dogwood bushes was actually a small part of what on second glance appeared to be a long joining valley of its own. If the tall pines next to the homestead were orphans of a larger forest, then this whole area could have been the new-growth home of the great-great-grandbirds of the one in my game bag. The more I looked, the better I liked what I saw. The stream still had enough of a watershed to keep the edges luxurious in foliage and cover. Deep thickets of poplar were edged by other larger trees and an occasional spruce tree for cold-weather shelter. This was the center of a grouse paradise.

There had been only one (other) bird-hunting trout fisherman of note in my village. He was a lawyer, like myself, only now long dead. A picture of him standing in front of a string of assorted grouse, ducks, prairie chickens, and woodcock was the sole remaining mark of his presence. My father, also a lawyer, came to this town at the end of the man's career. Years later I found some documents drafted by the man and walked down the hall to ask my father if he had known him.

"Yes, I did," he had replied. Then he added as an afterthought, punctuating it with a long puff of cigarette smoke: "He could never really bend his mind to the law, but, on the other hand, he killed a helluva lot of birds."

Yes, I thought, *and the Law, sir, is an ass.*

There was a small slot on the back of the watch, just enough for a fingernail to pry up the cover. It popped open with a snap.

"E. Howard Watch Co., Boston," it said in a line of block letters around an inscribed circle. In the middle, written in engraved script, were the words: "To Eugene, from Father, July 15, 1912."

It was his.

The photograph showed a soft-faced man wearing rimless glasses. Both of his slender hands were resting upon the barrel of a square-backed semi-automatic, which he had handled with unmistakable competence. Stretched between two trees and three other companions was the combined bag of fifty-six grouse, ducks, prairie chickens, and woodcock. The picture was part of a display in the city hall. I looked at it from time to time when I was there on business or attending a city council meeting.

I had found his mother lode.

It was a short walk through the dry humps of grass, past the old stumps, across the creek, and over to the pasture corner. A strip of mixed hardwoods and dogwood berries ran up to the house. Dixie's tail wagged furiously as she trailed a scent ribbon into the thickest of the clusters. The leaves were still thick in the understory and in the treetops, but not enough to cover the escape of two grouse that broke out from her rush. The first one saw the movement of my shotgun coming up and flared to the right, losing enough speed in the turn that I was able to roll it over in the air with my first shot. I was quick on the slide in those years and this was a lightweight Remington 31, the smoothest pumpgun ever made, but I was not fast enough to catch up to the second one. It swung out over the field and flew the woods' edge up to the house.

Dixie brought me its companion, which I put in my vest as we followed up the flush. The house was square, in two stories, with a dormer coming out of the side of each roof slant and the peak ends bobbed off in the Dutch style. Wood shakes covered the walls and roof. There was a clump of lilacs by the front door, and to the side, in true settler fashion, was the plum grove. I paused to look in the window. The house was deserted and had been so for a number of years. There was a pile of *Saturday Evening Post* magazines on the table by the window, the top one dated 1963.

I had waited too long for the liking of the second bird. It had settled into the lilac bushes by the front door, and seizing the opportunity presented by my nose pressed to the window, it roared out behind me and banked around the back of the house and was gone.

I sounded off with a loud exclamation of surprise and straightened up, banging my head on the top eave. I suppose Dixie heard the commotion and decided, given the volume and punctuation, that she was in trouble. She came around the front and huddled down in the grass to let the storm pass.

Which it did. Rubbing the new knob on my head gently, I continued to explore the surroundings.

The house was set into one of three small hills. The front was level with the farm field, facing the creek. Behind the house it sloped sharply downhill, allowing the door in the basement to open out to the drive that was cut into the next hill. On the left was the third hill, covered with woods. In the field beyond that stood a fine tall barn.

It was a perfect setting, with small openings separated from the house by woodlots, and a big main field right out the front door.

Since the wooded hill was in the rear and also in the general direction the lilac bird had flown, I walked through the tall backyard grass, onto the driveway, and entered the treeline by a path which left the drive. The evening was coming on by this time.

I didn't see the headstone right away because it was not cut granite. It was just a gray field-rock standing up on end with an unusual necklacelike ridge around its top. When I got closer I could see the frost had knocked down the remaining green parts of a cluster of tiger lilies. Then I saw the footstone. It was small and rectangular with deep-cut lettering in a modern design. I brushed the leaves and grass aside to read the inscription there.

"Laura Pedersen," it read. "Born 1881, died 1898."

This was indeed the old Pedersen home.

Some lands are flat and grass-covered. Others are water-worn with deep cuts and rocks thrust into the sky. In some places the world is deep in three-tiered jungle or perched on the edges of mountain cliffs. But if magic exists anywhere in the world it is here.

When my son was just a little baby he had a restless night. I was holding him quietly, sitting before a lowering fire in the library of my home. I became aware of a warmth beyond the fire and his small being. With this came a murmuring, not of any spoken word, exactly, but more of that rustling approval from an assembled people, my people, my lineage. It was a welcome, a spiritual applause to his entry into this world.

I stood up from the stone and, involuntarily, took off my hat. I was filled with that same essence, surrounded by the warm flow of this place.

It was going to be a long walk back to the old car. For a while I had been in a dimension far from this one, so when I reached the drive I looked for the old house with the anxiety that it might not be there. It was, of course, and so also all the landmarks I needed to get home.

In the years that followed the discovery of the pocket-watch farm I used it as a touchstone for new directions and, more than once, for quiet reflections. My parents gave me a Rolex watch when I graduated from high school. I wore that watch through college, the army, my tour in Vietnam, and law school. It was on my wrist right until a hot brushy chase after a covey of grouse that had flown downhill into the grassy bottom surrounding Wood Row Creek. As I sat on a log puzzling over how they had disappeared I looked down at my wrist to discover the time. The watch was gone.

It is a stainless steel Oysterdate. If you find it, you'll see it's engraved on the back:

"To Ted from Father, June 4, 1965."

Keep it, and go across the creek; the gravesite is on the hill behind the house.

Chapter 3
Middle Sea

A tuning fork is a small, lowly instrument that, when struck, gives forth a perfect note. Entire symphonies can be composed around its single, clear reference. This phenomenon belongs not just to music. Consider how teams are formed around one player of extraordinary talent, or cities built in a certain location. The Pedersen farm creek bottom is such a place.

The course of Wood Row Creek takes a sharp turn at the farm's far corner. The stubborn rocky side of the ridges here causes it to pool for a moment and then flow along the side of the homestead, past the big pines, and into the cut which, through eons of persistence, it formed in the soft center of one of the hills. This opening is not a canyon. (Minnesota lacks mountains, and therefore a frame of reference to describe a passage that is too small to be a canyon.) It is magnificent, however, in its small way. Boulders are washed in the headlong descent of the water and add music to the movement of the stream. The earth has gathered here and created a grove of trees. These, in their turn, have attracted the beaver.

There are as many kinds of dams as there are engineers. We have a small one in my town, created in the early 1900s to generate electricity. There's also the Hoover Dam. The beaver dam on Wood Row Creek is of the Hoover variety, and is best viewed from the downstream side, from which vantage you can fully appreciate its marvels. Four feet high on each corner, it stretches across the breadth of the creek to a center height of over eight feet. In high water the glistening edge of the pond brims the whole expanse.

But that year the water had not been high. The hay meadows upstream flood when the dam is in full repair, so the settlers and farmers have over the years pulled it apart to lower the water. If the price of fur is high the beavers are trapped out and the structure falls into disrepair. This ebb and flow of the pond makes fertile soil that catches the seeds spread by man and plants, and when the conditions are right a fine crop of buckwheat springs up on an inlet mud bar next to the upstream side of the pond. This was one of those years.

I had been hunting the grouse that lived in the edges of the old pastures, and following the dog and my own whims along the flowage I ended up at an old tractor that apparently had chosen to die in the middle of an opening. Its owner had left it there, in peace or frustration. Its contoured metal seat made a fine place to rest that particular weary part of my body, and I was admiring the subtle feathers of my last bird when I heard a furious quacking. My English setter Salty was still napping under the axle, but my Lab Dixie had slipped through the willows that surrounded the opening and scared up a flock of mallard ducks. I slipped out of the tractor saddle and joined her at the pond. There were still almost a hundred more ducks feeding on the crops that had volunteered to grow up on the mud bar.

This was a new dimension. The pond had occasionally held a duck or two that flushed when I crossed over the top of the dam in previous seasons. This year, however, the water was low enough to form a narrow beach along the pond side of the dam, and it was clear from the feathers and debris on the water that the place had become an important feeding point. It would be simple for me to drive my old car along the trail until I came to the opening, turn into it, and park next to the tractor. Then my retriever and I could sneak onto the dam before first light and be waiting when the ducks came in to feed.

It began as such things always begin, in the darkness of early morning. That time of day when yesterday's plan seems stupid, but so much effort has gone into getting this far that it is equally moronic to turn back. I had decided to make a day of it. My small white setter Salty, my bird-shooting vest, walking boots, and light clothes were stowed in the car. There had been a heavy frost overnight. I had brought a heavy brown sheepskin-lined coat, which together with a drab army blanket would be my blind. I had decided to sit on the pond side of the dam, wrap up in the coat and blanket, put my open-bored 12-gauge double across my knees, and wait for the ducks to come in.

It is interesting to consider what sort of creature leaves his warm bed for a wheezy, gassy old car and the company of two dogs. Such a thought occurs between shutting off the motor and opening the door. In the distance between the door and the back hatch on the old station wagon I remembered that one week ago I had met a young hunter at this very spot. He had been carrying a 30-06 rifle: "Hunting bears," he had said. A big one had been raiding the corn that he had planted in the Pedersen pastures. I had seen the evidence myself. The old raider had sat down on the edge of three rows, pulled them over himself, and had eaten his way to the top.

The little white setter was curled up into the side of my dear old black Lab Dixie. Pointing dogs were new to me then. I had only one kennel and the pup had seemed lonely, so into the door she went and from that day forward they were inseparable.

I pulled the side-by-side L. C. Smith from its case, put the blanket and heavy coat on the ground, and laid the gun on top.

"C'mon, Dixie, let's go. Salty, you stay; stay girl, we'll be back in a bit."

I eased the hatch down, drew up my hip boots, picked up the gun, coat, and blanket, and followed the dark little trail that my dog had cut through the frosty grass.

I stepped out of the willows and stopped for a moment at the edge of the dam. On the left was the earth wall, all grass covered, which ran the width of the valley, ridge to ridge. Below the dam was swamp grass and the stream rushing over the big stones into the trees. Above the dam, on my right, were three bands of color: the sky, now gray with first light; the black trees of the far ridge; and the flat, gray water, reflecting the morning light. There were no ducks. Where the water touched the mud it had frozen a perfect white line. There was no wind, just padding sounds of my feet and the quiet smoke of my own breath.

"Far enough," I said, glad for the company of my own voice. "Dixie, c'mon back, sit girl, and stay." I laid the blanket against the wall. I was about midway across the dam and directly in front of the icy top of the mud bar just peeking out of the water about fifty yards away. Putting the big sheepskin coat over my shoulders like a cape, I sat down on the blanket and drew it around my legs. The coat had a wonderful, high storm collar which I raised up to cover my neck. Then I leaned back against the grassy slope of the dam, put a load in each barrel, closed the gun, and rested it across my knees. Life was good.

I blew a long breath out into the sky just to watch the steam. Once, when I was a Boy Scout, we had camped out in cold weather. I had a wonderful sleeping bag. That night I had done the same thing many times just to enjoy the difference between the cold hard air outside and my soft warm den. Now little points of frost gathered along the cloth edge of my coat and small white stars grew on each bit of barrel dust. Dixie lay quietly at my feet facing the water, waiting for a cold swim. In a few minutes the ducks would be cupping into the pond.

"What the hell was that!?"

I was standing bolt upright in profound shock, the scream still echoing in my head. My shotgun was pointed at the dark trees. Dixie was standing, facing the same direction. She raised her eyes at my question, seeming to ask the same. It had been a sound, but also an expression. It had not been a question, or a bark—something had made an emphatic opinion in the wildest of terms.

It came again, this time farther away, below the dam, moving through the trees. I noticed a quiet clicking in my ears. It was my pulse returning to its rightful place inside my body. That scream had sent it out to the stars.

"It's a wildcat," I said. "Probably wanted to cross the dam and found us in the way. Sit down, girl." The blanket was no longer warm and the big sheepskin coat couldn't slow the shivers that ran up and down my back. "Helluva way to say good morning," I mumbled.

It was going to be a clear day; the sunlight was just touching the treetops. The sun was rising on my left, casting its early rays back toward the old car and the farmstead. The trees there were showing their yellow leaves around dark corners still in the shadows.

I heard Salty bark. It was slow and tentative at first, but it picked up into a frantic chorus. I could hear her voice changing as she moved around inside the car. Then I heard a low moan ending in a deep "woof." With that sound came a cloud of steam, shining in the sun, rising out from one of those dark holes in the foliage.

"Ooooh mother," I whispered, "it's the bear."

I saw its breath again, closer to the car, this time up high. It was standing on its hind legs, in the willow edge, trying to make sense out of the peculiar sight of a barking car.

"Ooooh Dixie, what if that thing decides to cross this dam?" I looked down. Her hair was standing out like quills along her back and hindquarters.

The edge of the water was only a foot or two away, but it was a sharp drop-off. This had been the deepest part of the pond at full flood. I figured that there was at least five feet of water and a couple feet of mud. I pushed my hip boots down below my knees, unsnapped the legging straps, and shook my feet loose. If that bad boy came walking down the berm, I was going for a cold swim.

In the meantime, Salty kept up her serenade. The bear blew out two big puffs of breath, sounding like an old coal-fired train engine.

Train engines, I thought, *I remember train engines.* They used to stop in town to refuel and let the passengers out for dinner at the hotel. When the engineers and firemen came across the highway they would bring the evening papers to the delivery boys. I had spent many a cold winter evening waiting in the light of the cafe windows for my papers. But I had never been so cold, or scared, as I was listening to that bristling steam engine.

The bear was gone, melted away—bored, I guess, or hungry for corn. I also melted, into a puddle of shaking ooze. The first ducks caught me unawares, bent over in relief, head down, with my gun across my knees. I noticed them only when I felt a mist on my face and heard the swish of their landing. It was too much for Dixie; she dove in after them and they were gone, up into the black middle band of trees and then out and away into the sky.

She swam back huffing and puffing, climbed out, and shook the cold water all over me. "Okay, okay, girl, I'm back in the game." I pushed my feet back down in the boots, sat on the blanket, and drew the heavy brown coat over my shoulders. Two or three more mallards were suddenly right over my head and then gone. They were coming into the pond with the black trees in the background. I couldn't see them until they were right on top of my head.

"That's the answer, Dixie!" If I could crunch down low on my hands and knees I could see more of the sky and less of the black treeline. I spread the blanket out over the mud and got down as low as I could without lying in it.

A single (perfectly black against the sky) came in over the trees and dipped down to swing over the dam. I rose up on my knees, swinging the grouse gun as I followed the bird's flight above my head. When it looked right I pressed the front trigger. The duck was stopped in midair and collapsed straight down into the water. Dixie was on it like Joe DiMaggio under a fly ball.

She swam back and trotted down the ice line, her tail swinging a happy spray of water.

"Tough luck, girl, we flopped a Suzy." It was a hen mallard. Now we had to wait for more light to be sure of our targets.

I suppose ducks have their reasons. Maybe something better was on the menu. There were no more customers, and an hour after sunrise it was too beautiful to sit on the grassy side of the beaver dam hoping for another flight. We quit, and rolling the coat and muddy blanket into a ball I carried that in one hand and the gun in the other. Dixie brought the duck and followed me to the car.

Salty was never one for big hellos, until that morning. We may have looked like the lost battalion of World War I, mud covered and discouraged, but to her we were the governor's pardon from her fate as bear breakfast.

One duck will never win first prize in a contest for best reward. It is almost a punishment. Only a masochist wants to clean just one duck. But it was a start, and the rest of the creek valley was before us, with the sun just at the top of the trees.

A short distance below the dam there is a big thicket of gray dogwood shrubs—the candy for all of grousedom. In season, those bitter little gray berries at the end of their bright red stems are sought out before all other forage. I have found patches of this brush used so intensely that the area stinks like a rancid bird cage. Salty is familiar with the plant and the fact that grouse like to hang out there. When her bell stopped only fifty yards from the car I knew she had found a bird to point.

"Heel, Dixie, heel," I urged as we quick-stepped to the cover. I could see Salty ahead of me, locked on point as tight as a fist. I worked my way to her right side, placing myself between the point and the streambed. When the bird flushed it would try to cross the water, putting the soft ground behind it to break up any chase.

I was close enough to watch Salty's eyes. Her gaze was locked straight ahead and low. Perhaps this was a woodcock. That would be right in the scope of a one-duck day. Timber-doodles get in the way of grouse hunting. Shooting one is like kissing your sister. It's a kiss, but it won't keep you awake at night.

The bird was up and away, arching for the clear air over the swamp grass. Some birds are shot after a long look and a careful calculation of the lead; others are shot dead in the air, just a heartbeat before the trigger is pulled. A shot like that is all instinct. It never misses. This was one of those times. No intellect involved, it was a merging of eye, hand, and machine...and it was a woodcock.

Dixie, the master marker, was on her way to find the spot. However, Salty was still on point!

I love it when a gun has ejectors, I thought as I opened the action. It's a small thing, but there is just something exhilarating about watching a smoking empty fly across the brush tops while you dig for a loaded shell. I closed the gun and pushed through the last ten yards of dogwood in front of Salty. This time a grouse came up beating the last few stems out of its way and trying for the yellow cover of a poplar stand just a short dive away.

Bad luck for the bird. A rising left-to-right shot is one of my favorites; in a puff of feathers Dixie had something else to find.

A grand slam. One duck, one woodcock, and one grouse mixed liberally with the essence of bear, danger, wildcat surprise, and served up in one place. Truly a symphony, tuned by location and played out...in several movements.

Chapter 4

The Cartway of Time

Time passes in one direction only. Its door swings open and things go through it, but a man cannot return across any threshold except his own. All that remains of the past of others are the things they left behind.

There is the foundation of a grand house built into a hillside just downstream from the Pedersen farm pond. South facing, its remains are a Stonehenge collection of poured concrete walls and window openings. The wood for a dwelling of this size was not cut from those waist-high stumps above the beaver dam. It was milled in town and hauled out here, where it was formed into a fine frame house with a spacious porch from which its owners could enjoy the view of the little valley and its tumbling brook. A great meadow must have stretched out from the streambank, rising to meet the woods' edge that crested the high ridge. I know this because the trees all along the ridge are old oaks, but those from the oaks back to the brook and up to the ruins are younger trees and almost all poplar.

That is how I found this homesite and the old road. When I say "old road" I am not referring to it in the sense of time. What I mean is the way it came to be formed by the hills and streams that it was made to cross. When the township supervisors got enough money they abandoned it for the "new" road, which is now a grass-centered mud-rut trail right down the section line.

"One day is one mile." That was the township rule in those days. The Caterpillar that made it was a big one with an engine that could only be started by putting a crowbar into its flywheel hole and yanking the crankshaft over until it caught hold with a cough and roar. Then it was four passes after the trees were cut. One down each side to lay the earth to the middle, and one more on each side to crown it up. The road was made along the town line to the corner that now is my landmark to turn and park next to the old wrecked tractor, a Minneapolis Moline in its younger and better days.

A cartway is one rod wide, sixteen and one-half feet. There were a lot of them in the early days of this land. They were the trails that connected one homestead to another, and they wound between the hills or around them when necessary. A cartway was part road and part game trail. When it came to a stream, a crossing called a low-water ford was constructed. Most of these were built by the timber companies to pull the logs out to the mill landings. The farmers and settlers adopted them as the easiest way to travel through the country. Neither the deer nor the teamsters went out of their way to cut through a hill just to keep a straight line.

I had flushed a bird from the weedy ditch of the town road on my way to the turnoff. The area was then unfamiliar to me, and when that is so, it is my practice to follow birds. What better guide to new and better grouse hunting than a native? The bird had flown into a cluster of poplar sprouts which formed the edge of a grassy opening. I parked the old car, shrugged on my vest, and turned out my Lab Dixie. The edge turned downhill, and from this vantage I could see spread out before me the lower reaches of a flooded meadow and the high oak crest of the ridge that turned the flow of Wood Row Creek.

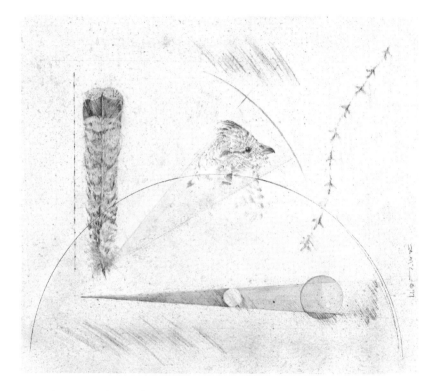

About midway down the hill was a copse of old pines and some newer trees gathered in one spot. On the right of this, glowing in the sun, were two bright red apples. A singular sight for Minnesota, and especially so in late October. The grouse was now forgotten for a crisp red apple on a golden fall afternoon. I ate one, put the other in my pocket, and threw the core to the dog. Next to me, Dixie loved two other things in all the world: the first was retrieving; the second was eating anything that did not eat her. These were big apples and it was an old tree; with visions of eastern grouse shooting in my head I explored around the nearby corners and niches.

A fire had consumed the wood parts of the house and had probably at the same time opened the hard-sealed cones of the nearby pines, because their small grove was in reality the basement or root cellar of the home. I walked around in front of these, and there facing the valley were four tablets of cement. They were window openings without the wood cap at the top. Tombstones for a house now crumbled into its own grave.

In the meantime, Dixie had been busy scuffling and snuffling after the bird. A whir of wings made me turn around in time to watch the grouse sail downhill. It turned sharp right to fly into an archway in the trees.

I kept my eyes fixed on that spot and walked quickly toward the woods' edge. The grass was high. I stepped into a small ditch in the same way, and with the same grace, that one misses the last step in a staircase.

I was standing on an old roadbed. It started at the hilltop, curved past the dooryard of the home, and disappeared in the dim light of the arch, traveling down to a small creek that ran into the larger flow of the little river. I walked down the raised portion of the trail, my stomach twisting with the pleasant tightness that occurs in anticipation of a new adventure.

The heavy field grass couldn't live in the shade of this place, but the ferns could. The frost had taken them down and spread the fronds out in a carpet of dark brown stretching across the lane from one old ditch to the other. About midway between myself and the far mud bank of the little tributary, a black log lay across the trail. Dixie snuffled and scuffed through the dry debris until she was standing in the creek. She walked along in the water, lapping up its flow, swinging her tail happily from side to side.

Among her other fine qualities, Dixie had a very expressive face. There is always some speculation in giving human qualities to dog behavior, but I think that an animal can express surprise as well as any man. Dixie jerked her head up and at the same time raised her eyebrows with a grunt. There, on the creek bank, stood a grouse snapping its tail open and shut in agitated display. She was never much of a bird watcher. In about the time it took her to draw in the required breath, she was bursting out of the water in pursuit.

The grouse was up off the ground, grabbing for the air between the dog and the overstory of ash trees. Straight up it climbed, and I followed its flight with the swing of my shotgun until the barrels went past its head. I shot, but the bird just staggered for a slight drop, then it surged up again, reaching higher and higher for the space above those shadows on the ground. I followed it and pressed the back trigger. The recoil of the gun carried my leading hand past the climbing grouse in a gesture as if to say: "After you, Alfonse."

He stalled, and in a perfect Immelmann turned on his wing to bank back toward the ground. He must have died at about that moment, for he lost all control and, spinning in a slow spiral, fell into the treetops. From there he bounced from limb to limb until, disdaining all contact with the ground, he hung himself in the crotch of a branch, swinging back and forth beyond the reach of the dog.

"This one would have smoked the last cigarette to a stub and spit at the firing squad, Dixie." I slipped the bird into my game pocket. "Let's follow this old road and see if he has any brothers."

The rivulet was hardly more than a short hop to the other bank but it had patiently worked its will on the roadbed until the cut was deep enough to let the water into the main flow of Wood Row Creek. The homesteader had raised enough earth to allow me to climb out of the little valley and along the side of the main ridge. Here the beaver had done their work, clearing the trees to build the big dam now in sight upstream. The gray dogwood bushes had filled in the sunlit opening from the tributary's valley to the dam. Great trees blocked my way, felled by the beavers but too big to drag into the water. I climbed up on one trunk in order to step over to another, and in this manner made my way toward the little opening where the tractor lay. From time to time a grouse was flushed by Dixie, who was out somewhere ahead of me but invisible in the underbrush. There was no chance for a shot, for I was always out of balance or under an over-hang. Finally, panting for a breath and swearing revenge against the clan, I rested on the steel saddle of the old tractor.

There are the ruins of a deer shack in a spruce grove close by. Another man's land cuts into the long edge of the Pedersen holding, not unlike a brick in a staggered wall. The very corner of the tract is adjacent to the tractor, and it was here the cabin was built, close to water and the road. Because of its proximity to the road, the little house was vandalized and its walls torn out. Within a few years the rest of the front collapsed into the basement hole and it became a haven for porcupines, bears, and the like.

If the birds flew straight along the creek they might have settled near the old ruins. So, with that in mind, I sent the dog on ahead and took the path that would bring me past the open end. She seemed awfully interested in the part that was collapsed in front. Her tail was wagging furiously as she pawed and whined to find a way in.

I stepped up quickly, grabbing her collar to keep her away from what I assumed was a skunk or a prickly tail. It was neither polecat nor porcupine. Inside the ruins, walking about on the floor, were three grouse.

The first to start upright was the nearest bird. In the next second it was flying straight up through the hole in the cabin roof like a feathered bottle rocket. This startled the other two and they split in two directions, one out the broken window, and the other out the door, passing close enough to touch my nose with its wingtip.

I was already somewhat off balance trying to stand bolt upright with a seventy-pound Lab in my hand, and I was dumped on my backside when Dixie seized the opportunity to lunge at the bird closest to my face.

Some years later I would relate this story to Arthur Pedersen, who responded in his Norwegian brogue: "Vell, you know dat der is two tin plates in dat front vindow of our house? Yah, und I come up to dat vindow ven der was only one pane broke, und I say vut is dis? I look in dat vindow und der in duh house is a pat'ridge. He is valking here and der. Und he sees me. Und he takes uff right thru anutter vindow. You tink he would use dah same vun. Yah, sure."

Arthur was speaking of the second house, which was built about 1920. The first one was on a hilltop near the creek. The same cartway that I was tracing through the lowland wound its way close to the deer shack ruins, through a small pasture, past the site of that second house, and close to the big barn, then turned along the edge of the hill to find its way to the foot of what is now an enormous white pine. Here, there was a bridge built on rock pilings. It is all gone now, but when I first found it the planks were still there.

On the far side of the bridge the roadbed is soft with the remains of old corduroy logs and a dense alder run leaning over the sides to shade out the sun. It is a heavy, wet, slippery jungle of vines and leaves. This is the home of the Bridge Bird.

Chapter 5
The Bridge Bird

It is a funny thing what the brain will do with memories. In the right place they become organized, as if it wants to take some meaning out of them, make a design, create a bridge between them, and weave a tapestry uniquely its own. If a man never returned to any one place, such a fabric would be long and narrow. It would become like a ribbon, each day tacked on and woven only from one end to the next. But I have been to the Bridge covert many times over the years, long enough to have seen the old span rot and crumble into the fast brown water, and long enough to walk the bark off the trunk of the old pine that fell across the stream when the bridge was gone. I never thought of this as a lucky event. The Bridge Bird wants me here. I know the sort of watch he keeps on me.

He wants me to cross over the water. If I stayed on the high side he couldn't draw me into the alders hanging over the trail. He wants me to walk out into the soft green ground that hides the boot-topping sinkholes. I didn't know a man could move around out there until the year Mike McIntosh was lured out.

If a man could hover like a hawk over this place he would see that upstream it is wide and wet with beaver ponds and flowages. Downstream it has the hard edge of the woods on one side and the soft flat pasture on the other. Willows have grown up in deep clusters wherever the current dropped enough black mud. Right at the bridge, however, the ground is like the narrow part of an hourglass, the hill on one side, the raised old bed of the cartway on the other. On both sides of the old road the alders have grown and spread their limbs, and creeper vines are wound in and out and around each other.

Mike and I had stayed on the little hill that is one side of the bridge. We had rested there with our backs pressed against the big white pine that was both landmark and toll guard. The grassy slope of the side hill invited a stroll in the late afternoon sun. We had almost gotten to the old spring house (the 1890s version of refrigeration) when a grouse flushed off the slope, setting its wings in a slow dive, and turned into the gloom of the alder bottom.

"I'm going to follow that one," Mike said, and before I could raise a question his orange cap was bobbing up and down in the yellow-and-green alders. I couldn't make out the whole progress, only the noises. The long groans as he ducked under one limb, only to have to step up on another. The short snappy barks when first one foot went under and then the other. All this time there were the chopping cuts of grouse wings beating back the twigs and flying across the creek to the other side. No shots, just the moaning groan of the human machine mired down in nature's monkey bars.

"Mike," I called, "are you coming out? I think the grouse have flown."

"Where is out?"

"Go downstream, try to make it to the old road," I replied.

"Hell, I'll just sit down and float under the bridge."

I look on this covey as the grouse equivalent of the Mafia. The Society of the Black Wing or somesuch. Other birds might be noble, honest, straightforward; some might even hold for the dog. Not this gene pool. The dead ones are those they send out to lure the hunter in.

Such was the first bird my little white English setter Salty ever pointed. Salty was two years old, unfocused, lean, and hard-running. That day I was hunting with two other companions, both older gentlemen, with pointing dogs—a Brittany spaniel and a large and regal English setter. The big setter had swung off to the right, crossing under the big pine and drawing his master along the hillside. Salty and I crossed the bridge, closely followed by Jerome and his little Brit. We heard a shot and turned to look back at the hillside. There was nothing further.

"Maybe he shot his dog," Jerome said. (It had been a difficult morning.)

"No," I replied, "then it would have been two shots."

We both laughed and turned to walk into the alder arches.

"You have a point." I heard Jerome say it at the same time I saw it with my own eyes. My first point, the first one from the first pointing dog I ever owned—the first base hit, the first touchdown; my kid had become a hero. The tall grass and creeper vines gathered around her like the fake green floss in Easter baskets. There she was, tail high, head down and turned, right front leg lifted. I stepped up beside her, the bird came up perfectly and fell dead at the shot. Somewhere out in the depths of the bog the Bridge Bird nodded and said "He has the bait," then set the hook.

To hunt with a pointing dog is to make this commitment: wherever the dog points, you will go. If not, be mindful of the old story of the hunter finding the skeleton of a dog pointing the skeleton of a grouse. Sometimes, in the next ten years or so, the Bridge Bird would occasionally lose its bet. Salty was a smart dog, and if her situation was truly impossible she seemed to sense it and would rush the bird to tree it. Then, if that was successful, she would bark "treed" until I came to her. But one part of it was always true: I still had to come.

I know the sort of watch he keeps on me.

Most of Wood Row Creek runs through the Bridge covert like water seeps through a sponge. Etched into the top of that sponge is a twisted rivulet of running water. You have heard of a game called a three-legged race. In the Bridge covert one man and a shotgun provide the only contestant. Two legs, one always balanced on a long springy alder whip, and the other either going into or coming out of a soppy hole. One hand gripping another alder tree and pulling forward, the other holding the bird gun free of the tangled vines. All this to seek the bird that was pointed in some impossible mess, by a small, white, determined dog.

"Where is it, girl?"

Behind you, idiot, says the Bridge Bird as it whirs out to show just enough of a blur to prove that the dog had it perfect and the failure was mine.

I suspect—though I cannot prove—that the Bridge Bird colony keeps sentries on the edge, especially near the big marking pine. Their job is to leave enough scent floating in the air. This draws the dog across the creek and into the tangle. The walk to the bridge itself is made across an open pasture so the dog naturally runs ahead and the hunter lets it go because, after all, there are no grouse in a grassy field. When the hunter reaches the bridge he has no dog. He pauses for a while. The dog does not return in its usual fashion.

"I must have a point," he says to himself or to his companion.

"Where?"

When a hunter thinks of a "point" in other places he thinks of something in addition to what is already there. Grass, bushes, trees, a bird, and a dog on point. In the Bridge covert there is no dog. The "point" is not something that is there, or really anywhere. It is not a presence; it is an absence. Look around, nothing has changed. Same place, same guy, same gun, same alder mess—but no dog. I get the same feeling when I stand at the shore of Lake Mille Lacs. I can't see the other shore. There are thousands of walleyed pike in front of me...but where?

I know the sort of watch he keeps on me. It's *"Come into my web," said the spider to the fly.*

I suppose every hunter handles this differently. The temptation is to walk along the hillside and peer into the leafy pile hoping to catch a glimpse of a blood-tipped tail, of the straight white line of the dog's back. Vain hope here. But I do what must be done. I do the same thing that every relief pitcher does when the count is three and two and the bases are loaded. I hitch up my pants, push my cap back, pull it down tight, spit, and step into the windup.

One would think that, after all these years, I would have found an easier way in and out of this place, but I haven't. It reminds me of this old exchange between the hunter and the guide.

Hunter: "Where are we?"

Guide: "Lost."

Hunter: "How do you know?"

Guide: "Every time I have been lost it looked just like this."

Technology has produced the dog beeper. I don't use one myself; whenever I hear that sound I keep expecting to see the rear end of a front-end loader backing out of the underbrush. It wouldn't help here anyway. In fact, if the Bridge Bird knew about beepers and could get a few, he would stash them out in the places that he wants to draw me into. He doesn't need them. He just perches on a tall bush above the electric dog and waits for the owner. He probably likes them better than Salty's bell because they avoid all the suspense over whether I can find the dog this time. Some of the men I hunt with use beepers.

In the Bridge covert, the beeper adds a whole new, and modern, dimension to the absent dog. Now the hunter can hear the dog even though he cannot see him. He is being paged. The Bridge Bird not only has hidden the dog but is applying stress to the hunter. Well, he isn't applying stress, the guy is doing it to himself. He knows the rule: "I point, you come and find me." The beeper adds that modern touch: "Right Now!"

I tricked that bird Mafia once. I walked in from the other side and slipped up to the bridge through the green alder tunnel. Then, Salty and I stepped into the little grass landing opposite the hillside and the big pine. We were on their side of the bridge and they didn't know it. Panic and confusion reigned; a covey of seven swarmed away in a flurry of wings, leaving two behind, one in the water and the other fluttering in the sunny patch under the pine. My happy old Lab Dixie cleaned up the casualties, but it never happened again.

There is always a Bridge Bird, and that is what keeps me coming back. But this year Salty stayed home. It was Saturday of the second weekend. My son was with me, and my new pup, Beans, a German shorthair. Two years before this season I had started another English setter to replace Salty.

She was a speckled goddess of speed, and is tearing the top off some Missouri bean field even as I speak. But she was too much dog and a race car in an off-road game. I never brought her here to the Bridge covert; it would have been like piling brush in the path of a cruise missile. Beans is different. He is German and never leaps without looking first.

Salty finished her work last season with a grouse hunt on the day after Christmas. Two pups, Beans and my son Max, had yet to begin. The three of us had worked through the Pedersen farm, sat in front of the old house, visited Laura's grave, and then crossed the tall grass pasture to the big pine. Max and I stood on the rock pile that was one end of the bridge and watched the current turn the yellow leaves around and around. I gestured toward the fallen tree trunk that was now the crossing. And there stood Beans...on point. I could only say one word—"Max"—before a great brown-tailed grouse rose up out of the weeds, arching over the point and our heads. His flight spanned the old bridge site to cross the creek.

Two shotguns spoke as one, and he dropped, his head thrown back, his tail spread out in the sun. He lay there in the small open grass just at the far end of the other side. Beans stepped into the creek to swim across, then thought better of it, came out again on our side, and, without a word on my part, hopped up on the fallen pine. He crossed over to the other side, picked

up the great bird, and crossed back. The circle was closed, but I didn't know it then. I was lost in the tumult of the moment.

"It's the Bridge Bird, son!"

"Awesome, it's huge!"

I turned it over and over in my hands and passed it to Max. We gave each other high-fives and other congratulations reserved for things like first touchdowns and first base hits, and of course, first points. We quit right there and went home.

Salty met the truck when we drove in and I showed her the big bird. She snuffled it a few times and hopped off to the back doorsteps; the arthritis had crippled her hind legs. When I walked out of the house to finish putting things away I found her lying in the flower bed, something she never did.

"C'mon, girl, time for supper." She did not get up.

She was stone deaf, a new malady, so I bent down and ruffled her ears. She did not stand up. She couldn't move her hind quarters and one front leg was held out stiff. I scooped her up in my arms and she cried out slightly. I knew then what I should have known at the Bridge.

I laid her back down in the flowers and went into the house to the kitchen, where my wife and the kids were standing.

"I want each of you to say your good-byes to Salty; she has decided to leave us," I said, and called the vet. He and I talked briefly. "A stroke, perhaps a seizure, but, you know, with a dog as tired as that one..." Yes, I knew.

I carried her out to the truck and placed her on the seat next to me. Then I went back into the house, picked up my game vest, and took out the Bridge Bird. I snipped off one of his wings with the game shears and placed it in my pocket, walked back out to the truck, and drove the half-hour between home and the clinic.

The rest of the story is familiar enough to every dog owner, with this difference. When she slipped away I held the Bridge Bird's wing under her muzzle so that she would have as her last sense of life the essence of what gave it meaning at the start. His wing was her bridge into the next world. He wanted it that way; I know the sort of watch he keeps on me.

Chapter 6

Sporting Goods, Row Three

When I walk into a room, the picture that is tilted slightly attracts my attention. It is out of place, disorderly, or at least unusual. It is my legal training, I guess, to focus on that which is out of line, not logical. I always straighten the picture. My wife, on the other hand, leaves it alone and more often than not comments on the colors or how lovely the image is.

That is how I came to find the windrow coverts. They didn't make sense. Their rough, wild, brushy appearance was out of place with the orderly pasture that surrounded them, and it attracted my attention.

After the bridge over the creek is crossed, all that remains of the old cartway is a wide path through the woods. It climbs the side of the creek valley and bends over through a strip of new-growth poplar to wind its way through a hardwood forest parallel to the run of Wood Row Creek. I used to trace its course through those woods, and in the early years I shot a fair number of grouse along the way. But the trees were mature when I first found the line of the old road, and the woods have since become stale.

I followed the clustered mess of the poplar in the grown-up strip one day just to see where I would come out. I was paralleling the old cartway, walking it with a hunting companion, when he yelled a warning that a grouse was coming my way. When a grouse is moving really fast it cuts through the overstory like a delta-winged jet. I heard this bird coming before I saw it. It had its wings tucked in tight and it was in a long dive, clipping the twigs of tree branches as it passed high in front of me. I swung through it but not far enough, for when I fired the bird cartwheeled end over end in a broken-wing spin to the earth.

My Lab Dixie was with me that day and close enough to watch the bird fall. She took off without a command, and I opened the double, sat on a log, and dug around in my pocket for my pipe and matches.

"Did you get it?" my partner asked.

"I got enough of it for Dixie," I responded. I thought about how fortunate I was on occasions like this. My dear old retriever had brought back several birds over the years that had shown no sign of any hit at all. This one was as good as delivered.

After a few minutes I heard a screech of barbwire being dragged over a fence staple. I didn't know there was a fence anywhere in this piece. A bit more time passed and I relit my pipe. Then I heard the scuffle of her feet on the dry leaves and she appeared with the bird in her mouth and a bright red drop of blood on the top of her head.

"Did the grouse spur your dog's head?" my companion asked.

I looked her over closely as I took the bird. "No, it looks like a small wire cut."

The bird was minus some tailfeathers and somewhat rumpled from a chase through heavy cover. I dispatched it quickly, confirming with a twist of my fingers that except for a broken wing-knuckle the bird was entirely my dog's effort, and very little my own.

"I think there is a fenceline about three or four hundred yards up that line of small poplar regrowth." With that, I swung us away from our usual walk down the traces of the old cartway and up the hill toward the direction that Dixie had come from.

The poplar tangle ended at the corner of a cow pasture that had been cut out of the woods by a Caterpillar's blade. The driver had made long passes, each time laying the brush and trees up in lines and leaving the middle open for clover seed and grass. There were perhaps ten to twenty of these windrows from one side of the forty-acre opening to the other.

It had been done several years ago, and the man had not followed through with the usual custom of burning the piled debris, because new growth had sprouted between the log piles. Each windrow was a chaos of poplar trees about ten to fifteen years old, brush, gray dogwood bushes, and berries of all kinds. It was as if a game-bird biologist had planted long strips of grouse cover, and a golf course architect had laid fairways in between.

While I was scratching my head over this contradiction, my little white setter Salty came out of the woods on my left and stopped for a moment. Just long enough, apparently, for her Missouri quail genetics to kick her into overdrive. She swept down one side of a windrow, pouring speed into muscles that had been cramped by the slow going of heavy-brush grouse hunting. Her head was high and she was riding the slip streams of a thousand wonderful scents. Her steady friend and retrieving assistant, Dixie, stood by my side slapping the leg of my hunting pants with her tail.

Salty paused a moment to look back. I waved her on; twenty trips up and down each side of a forty-acre windrow was more dedication than I had at that moment.

"Let's walk along the wooded side and let her run the rows," I said. We were on the north side and the sunshine was warming the edge. It would be a perfect place for a bird to loaf on a late October afternoon.

Salty was a grouse dog—that rare individual, among thousands, that knew the quirky ways of the partridge. A quail is a gentleman and will stay out when asked. A woodcock spends so much time with its bill in the earth that I guess it just hates to leave it. But a grouse is a nervous little old lady shopping a white sale. It won't hold for anything less than a salesclerk willing to follow with a pad and pencil. Salty had that follow-them-to-hell persistence.

It is a custom among pointing dog trainers to insist that the dog stand until released once the point is made. Salty had the great fortune of having me as a trainer and I was not aware of this nicety—and quite a few others. When people ask me if I train my own dogs I acknowledge that I do, and quickly add that I don't know what is expected of a fully trained dog. I just know what I expect the dog to do, and train it accordingly. I can't take much credit for Salty though; she knew by instinct just how far to push a pointed grouse. Her manner when she got the scent of a bird was not to find and point it so much as it was to handle it. I learned to trust her and stay out of her way until she had it nailed down.

Sometimes, on rare occasions, I had the opportunity to see this with my own eyes. She would be locked up on a solid point, her body tight as a fist. About ten yards in front of her would be the grouse, often looking back. It would begin to walk away; she would move forward, just so, and the bird would stop. She was stalking the grouse like a cat, not to pounce on it, but rather to stop it and hold it for me. If I walked alongside her she would roll her eyes back to glance at me and say, eye to eye, "Be careful." Dixie was a compulsive flusher, on her own, but when Salty had a point she could freeze that old Lab with a glance.

This time it was Salty's body that was frozen—into a point. She was locked down about halfway up the side of one of the last three windrows. I gestured to my partner and we half-ran and half-walked up to that point, almost afraid to believe that a cagey game bird like the grouse could have gotten itself in such a spot. The strip was only about ten to twelve feet wide, and this particular location had a heavy understory of gray dogwood shrubs with a couple small hardwood trees nearby. On both sides the grass was close-clipped pasture about fifty feet wide. My partner had slipped through to the other side and was coming up to place himself in front of the dog and the cover.

I was at Salty's side, and at that moment a grouse flushed out of the tangle, banking right and curving out over the wide, open fairway. I had very little time to think about it, but time enough. I slid my finger to the back trigger of my double and touched it when the barrels swung ahead of the bird. The bird fell from a puff of feathers, bounced once, and rolled into a lump on the short green turf. At almost the same moment my bird was rolling to a halt, a shot came from behind me, followed by a second shot.

I turned around. Four grouse were rising to land in the nearby maple tree and my companion was frantically reloading. So was I.

"Did you get that one, Bill?" I asked.

"Yeah, yeah, what now?"

Dixie was bringing back my bird and Salty was still on point. One of the roosting birds lost its stupidity and dove out toward my partner.

BANG! BANG! "Damn!" and two spent hulls streaked across his shoulder.

"Can you believe this?" he whispered. "They just sit there!"

No, I couldn't. If someone had been telling this as a story the next part would have been the old "I shot 'em from the bottom up so the dead ones wouldn't spook the others as they fell" legend.

The evidence was there in front of me. It didn't make sense, but I didn't have any trouble seeing the birds.

We have an agreement: Bill and I don't shoot them out of trees. We have had a lot of fun with this over the years, throwing sticks and laughing as the bird stretched itself out longer and longer, content to pick the moment all by itself. It is a hard shot even for a ready gunner. The bird dives out, drops, then levels out and pours on the speed.

"I'll shake the tree, you get the first shot," I said.

"Done, go to it!"

If you get into this situation always offer to shake the tree. All the advantage lies with the shaker. It places you on the inside of the drop and the shot becomes a rising straight-away.

Dixie was hopping from one foot to the other, my first grouse limp in her mouth. It would have to wait. I stepped inside the dogwood shrubs, forcing my way through the screen of low branches until I could just reach the tree trunk. With my shotgun held in my right hand by its pistol grip, I turned my back to the tree, all three grouse right above me, and gave the slender trunk a mighty shove.

I heard his shot but I didn't watch it. One of the three was just then rising after its first drop. I swung the gun up from below and touched the front trigger just as the barrels covered the bird. I didn't see any of the others, just that one falling and bouncing like the first one, closely followed by my Lab running over to it with one bird already in her mouth. "This will be a neat trick," I thought.

I glanced over my right shoulder. My companion was hotfooting it to the next windrow, pausing to pick up his first bird and reload his gun.

I would like to say that Dixie then placed the birds side by side, picked them up by their heads, and returned to heel. But that goes along with the grouse-shot-from-a-roosting-tree legend. She went over, dropped one, picked up the other, brought it, and ran back again for the first. Not fancy, not legendary, just workmanlike.

And yes, Salty broke point without a tap on the head, slipped through the shrubbery, and galloped over to the next row to help Bill.

We did the same thing again the next day and caught them out in the open just as before. As the years went by we tried this earlier in the season without success, and later with the same result—nothing. It was a peculiar event associated with the end of October and we came to speak of it as the Halloween Miracle. Nothing is predictable so far as grouse shooting goes, but this repeated itself four years running. Then the cows got too hungry—and numerous—and ate up or trampled the rows into submission.

The appearance of this place could put a bird hunter off his guard, if he didn't know that grouse would pick their way along the rows until they ended up out in the pasture. I mentioned Mike McIntosh earlier as being mired down in the Bridge covert. That was in his earlier years with me, when the prospect of shooting a grouse was higher in his priorities. The windrow coverts were discovered sometime after he had been to England for the first time. Therefore when we stepped out of the sticks and branches of the woods and out onto the green fairways, he breathed a sigh of relief and opened his sidelock double, balancing it on his shoulder in a pose that would become his trademark.

While Mike rummaged in his pockets for a pipe and a light, Bill stood next to the woodline and I walked out to the third windrow, as before. The point was out of sight over a small round hill and I thought that I could flush the bird back toward the two of them if I could get up above the dog and walk down on it.

I could do it. Salty held the bird and it rocketed away from me, getting to full speed and ripping along low to the ground.

"Your way-y-y-y!" I yelled.

There was a long pause—the grouse zipped over the top of the hill—then a short pause and a shot. That was followed by an exclamation of profanity and long guffaws from both McIntosh and Bill.

When I walked down the hill I could see Bill bent over in mirth and Mike standing with his gun, now closed, laughing and looking on the ground for his pipe.

"He heard you yell," Bill said, wiping his eye, "then he sort of turned slowly to see this brown missile coming down on him. Then all I could see was an explosion of pipe tobacco and frantic movement. The bird hit the woods and was gone."

There are three windrow coverts in the Pedersen vicinity. This one is the farthest south. I found the next one quite by accident, but because of my luck with the previous cover I recognized it as a cover with potential. The last one completes the circle and is the best of them all.

The land which lies north and east of the first windrow covert and east of the Pedersen farm and Wood Row Creek is a series of rolling hardwood hills, unconnected by any trail, and organized only by the long wet boundary of a cattail swamp. Cattails, when you see them, mean about a foot or two of water. It is sometimes possible to jump from hump to hump in a tamarack swamp, or a flooded ash grove, but cattails are water, plain and simple.

I was following a small covey that had flushed off the northeast corner of the windrow pasture and scattered out into the woods. More to the point, the birds were in a direction that I wanted to go anyway. The woods quickly became too mature for good bird cover. It was clear from the relaxed attitude of the dogs that this was just traveling country, good only for yellow leaves and blackberry scratches. But I was content to let the trip unravel for the same reason that the bear climbed the mountain or the chicken crossed the road...I wanted to see the other side. About midway in my walk I turned toward a small cluster of pines perched on the brow of a hill. There was a fine little valley of dogwood bushes right down below it. Both dogs were already there and working the edge of the patch with renewed interest.

Pine thickets pose a unique problem for a grouse hunter. It basically comes down to this: You can't shoot what you can't see. The space from the ground to about three feet high is empty. The rest of it is a green wall. A bird flushed from the dogwood grove made the pine trees before I could shoot. Both dogs ran up and into the pines, with Salty promptly going on point and Dixie scuffling around underneath. Salty didn't fix the old Lab with her evil eye, because she had no firm idea where the scent was coming from. I, however, knew, and there was nothing to do but shake my head and stand on the outside with my shotgun hanging in my hands. The birds were up in the pine boughs, as close as the next tree and as far away as the moon.

It all comes down to that commitment thing again. The dog points, you go to the dog. I hitched up my pants, turned my cap around backwards, and spit. I am six feet tall and I do not duck-walk very well or shoot effectively from a half-crouch.

"Easy, girl, easy, I'm coming." The first one whirred away on my left, and the quick half-spin to look for it startled another out of the branches over my head. I still had not seen a feather or even a flash. Then another went, and finally a fourth. Dixie ran out after them and Salty followed suit. When I came out on the other side I understood the clear advantage of four legs and a non-upright posture.

The effort wasn't wasted. I could see an opening in the trees about one hundred yards ahead. I made for it like a rescued coal miner.

It was another bulldozed clearing, but this one was not pastured. The work had been done on the side of a large hill with the windrows running along the contours about seven rows deep from the flat cornfield below to the woods' edge on top. It was smaller than the first by about half, and the space between the piles was filled with tall grass and chest-high weeds. Off to my right, to the east, I could see the dark tar ribbon of the county highway. This was the very end of the same hardwood ridge that faced the porch of the old homestead.

I started from the top and worked my way downhill, weaving a course along and between the rows. The clearing work had been done several years ago and had apparently been abandoned, for no use had been made of the land. The last two rows produced a woodcock, which I ignored, and two grouse, one of which lingered under the point long enough for me to take revenge on it for the pine hill low-crawl. When I came to the end of the last windrow there was no question that I had concluded right about the work being abandoned. The broken rusty hulk of an old bulldozer was resting quietly in the field corner. Its plow was rammed up against a rock, and judging from the vines grown in and around the carcass of the machine, it had been in this state of suspended animation for some years.

This became the Caterpillar Windrows.

Some places just wither away for no apparent reason, like small towns between prosperous cities. The Caterpillar Windrows never became anything more than a place to walk through on the way to the next one. Perhaps its hillside location just took advantage of gravity to pull a hunter's tired feet to the next stop. Sometimes it would produce a bird or two, but mostly I liked it because it had a grove of hard-rock maple trees on the far side. I never lingered long in the Caterpillar because I liked to walk under those maples and kick my feet through its yellow world of fallen leaves. I liked the way the dogs would run across the ground kicking up those perfect paintings and looking timeless and eternal in that yellow light.

I was drawn through it for another reason. My resting spot was at the corner of the next field and the next set of windrows. I called my resting spot the Six Pack Corner—not because there was a cold package of refreshments there, but for the opposite reason. The place was named in the same way that tall people are called "shorty" or fat people "bones." It was at that place I would have sold some of my soul and a lot of my property for one cold beer.

The covert next to it became known as Turner's Windrow, named after an old friend and long-time hunting partner. Places are named after people as memorials, and sometimes because the person created them. In this case, however, I named it after Spencer Turner because it was the perfect representation of hunting with the man himself. The trouble of going through it was worth the pleasure I got out of it every time.

Chapter 7
Turner's Windrow

Civilized man has used armor for centuries. As a helmet and breastplate, it has been useful in turning aside arrows and other missiles, deflecting sword blades, and avoiding other rude thrusts of life. Formed around a motor and driver, it can be a tank that flattens obstacles and smashes through walls.

My dear friend Spencer Turner is like that. Inside the armor of his pear-shaped body and ample waistline is an Olympic athlete driving a tank. His physical antics have puzzled his other friends from time to time. He is legendary for tipping over canoes, getting trapped in electric fences, and falling over for no apparent reason. But I know why this happens. Every once in a while the indestructible Olympic athlete behind the controls pops the clutch or hits the wrong button. Driving a tank is not the same as ballet dancing. Spencer Turner's life is controlled by a principal of physics: Objects in motion tend to stay in motion. The bright and agile mind peering through those eye slits might give his limbs the right command but it just takes a while for it to get executed.

The windrow covert I named after him is the same way. It has a great golden center surrounded by almost impenetrable armor.

It is simply made. At the base of the great oak ridge facing the old homestead, and between those oaks and the small prairie floodplain of Wood Row Creek, a farmer had spread out six long lines of hardwood trees and bulldozed debris. He had died shortly thereafter, and this place, like all the others, had grown up. No cattle grazed here to keep the small trees and bushes down. The dozer blade had not cut deep enough in the earth to sever the root structure in its topsoil. The young trees came in with such vigor that they shaded out the grass and weeds. Wherever it could gain a hold, gray dogwood reached for the sun and spread itself in clumps twenty to thirty feet wide. The blackberry brambles wound themselves in and around everything that held the newly-turned dirt. On each side, the log piles sprouted this natural barbwire between their round rails. It was a smorgasbord for grouse and a rich source of woodcock worms.

At the far end of it, opposite Six Pack Corner by a quarter mile and butted up against a lush lowland of tall green ferns, a lumpy swamp of mixed ash, poplar, and great rocks blocked the flow from the farm pond. Game trails intersected as deer passed from one side of the creek to the other. In the first part of fall the ferns, still green—sheltered from a frosty death by the dense yellow canopy of the mingled hardwoods—would brush against my waist.

There was, and still is, the great trunk of an ash tree fallen across the flow. Right next to it, on both sides, the earth of the creek banks has been dug up by deer pausing to drink or jump across. A man and a dog passing from the dry corner and fighting through the cover are led to this place by game trails as sure as a camel walks to a desert oasis. A bird hunter can sit on the tree and watch the water flow under him on its way through the open pasture to the brow of the homestead hill. A tired dog can lie down in the water and make his hunter wish he could do the same.

The golden heart of Turner's Windrow is protected by the bristling armor in the spaces between the piles, which makes it impossible to make more than one pass. Each windrow is worth a trip, but a man has to decide what he wants to hunt. The first row is closest to the grass field. Woodcock like it here. There are soggy seeps and holes that hold water. Earthworms burrow under the tall grass of the field, and an easy escape is open to a quick flush into the piles behind. The second and third windrows hold both grouse and woodcock. The rows further up the ridge have only grouse. The woodcock seem to turn aside before they get there, or maybe just tire out from all the jinking and diving it takes to wind into the depth of it.

Two men can split the difference, with one fellow going high and the other low, hoping to move the birds between them. More hunters and dogs allow a trip down each row simultaneously. The flushing and shooting, however, will reach circuslike proportions, with two or more dogs often chasing the same bird and new flushes confusing a riot of noise and whistles. Whether the number of hunters is two or ten, though, no one ever wants to try it twice in one day.

The piles are too tall to climb and the spaces between the logs are too wide. A crippled or dead bird can crawl or tumble down beyond reach. Joel Vance, a companion of Turner's, had shot a grouse, but the bird had escaped the first try of his Brittany spaniel and both animals had wormed their way to the bottom of a pile. Turner and I heard yelling, and after a climb over two rows we came on the scene. All we could see was two legs sticking out of the top of the pile.

"Joel, what are you doing?"

"Spence, grab my legs!" he said.

"Where are you?" Spence answered.

"In the pile, grab my legs!"

"Okay," Spence replied, "but first, what are you doing?"

"I'm stuck, the dog is stuck, and the bird is stuck!"

"Sort of an old lady that ate the fly kind of thing," I remarked.

Spence got about halfway up the pile and grabbed Joel's legs. This gave Joel enough leverage to back out. When his shoulders came out, he pulled back with his arms and in his hands were the back legs of his spaniel. In the mouth of the dog was a live and kicking grouse.

Spence Turner, Joel Vance, and Mike McIntosh all came as a package from Missouri. They had gotten in touch with an outdoor writer of their acquaintance in Minnesota, who in turn called a friend of his for a tip on bird shooting in my area. This man called me, for he had no real experience or places to hunt grouse or woodcock. At that time I was a solitary act. I had yet to acquire a taste for pointing dogs and double guns, preferring my black Lab Dixie, and a lightweight Model 31 Remington pump 12-gauge. And I still wore castoff parts of my soldiering years, most particularly my old jungle boots.

They wanted to hunt woodcock. I knew nothing about the bird except for a vague notion that it preferred wet places. I gave directions to such a location and agreed to meet them for lunch along an easy-to-find country road. When they arrived (in the veritable cloud of dust and noise that precedes them even today) I was both a hero and an expert. My tip had resulted in almost fifty flushes in about an hour and a half. They had waded directly into a newly arrived flock of migrants. It had been a point, shoot, and load event.

I took them to the tractor ruins from our lunch site. We worked through the farm and over to the Bridge covert.

We split up here, Spence and I following the creek and Joel and Mike heading off toward the first windrow cover. In about two hundred yards Spence was missing. I noticed early on that he had a disturbing tendency to veer to the left, but since he was on my left I decided to sit on a log and wait. His white setter, Samantha, came along presently and waited with me.

Shortly after, I saw the underbrush shaking from side-to-side and Spencer emerged, flattening all before him.

"That dog's on point!" he said.

I looked over at the setter, but never having seen a point before, I remarked, "Naw, she's just resting."

"That's a point!" And having so stated he walked in, flushing five grouse.

I was impressed, and stared with open-mouthed amazement as all but one spread out in the nearby underbrush. The tardy one sat in a tree.

I could have let him shoot it off the limb, but I didn't. I let him take it the old-fashioned way. I shook the tree and he earned it, and four others before we were finished. His Samantha was a born grouse hunter, and it was from her that Salty came to me in later years.

The windrow came to have Spencer's name for this reason: just at that point when all seemed lost, or flown, busted, and hopeless, things would work out. My daughter Tessa was the first of my kids to hunt birds with me. She was, and still is, a tireless companion. But luck was just not with us that year, her second season of following me and the dogs through face-slapping brush thickets and poor opportunities. Every day that I had a good outing she was off doing things that teenagers have to do. I wanted her to get some sort of a reward for her dogged persistence and unfailing cheerfulness. We were in the second windrow. Spence was over in the first, thinning out the woodcock.

"Bird's up!" he shouted, and I caught a glimpse of a grouse rising in a loop up from his side, clearly a easy shot. He didn't take it. The bird settled on our side, coasting into the middle of a cluster of young poplar. I had it marked.

"Okay, Tessa, here's your chance; there's a grouse right up ahead in a tree." A bird hunter with lots of years and game taken can afford to be philosophical. But philosophy is theory; a tired and discouraged kid is reality. This was a bird in the bush, and with any luck at all it would soon be one in the hand, her first.

I killed my first grouse on a misty late afternoon exactly one and a half miles from this place. My father and my brother were with me and we were road hunting from the cab of our old Willys jeep. My dad didn't make me walk for the first year and a half; he hardly ever walked at all while "partridge hunting," as he called it. Road hunting was a cultural icon. It was all people did when looking for the brown bird. Anyone who used a dog and walked through the brush was considered a few bricks short of a full load.

"There's a grouse, Ted!" The little jeep came to a halt and I tugged on the cab door, stepping out on the trail. I had an old Model 29 Remington 12-gauge duck gun, full choked, with a 30-inch barrel. In the dim light of that late afternoon I could just make out the pointy triangle of the bird, standing in the left rut and bobbing its head with each small step.

"Load your gun." I pulled the high-base paper shell (No. 6, written right on the end) out of my coat pocket. A Model 29 was a bottom-eject and bottom-load type of action. The shell went into the magazine tube. The bird stepped closer to the high grass next to the ditch.

"Hurry up, son, he's walking away."

The slide release was a button located on the side of the receiver. It was close enough to the trigger for a man's hand, but a boy had to push it down with his thumb.

Clatter-clack. It was loaded.

I was breathing through my mouth in little puffs of steam and my heart was clicking in the back of my throat. I had to walk up the middle of the trail, maybe two or three steps.

"Shoot it, Ted!" I heard my brother moan in frustration.

The barrel seemed as long as a prairie blacktop, but there was the partridge right at the end of the bead.

I pulled the trigger...nothing. The safety was on!

"Shoot!" BANG!

Just like that, struck down by lightning and Federal No. 6 shot, my first grouse was thumping its life out on the cool soil of a dark afternoon. All the way home I just sat in the back of the jeep staring down at my grouse, the most beautiful one in the entire world, laid out carefully on the polished steel floor of that old '47 Willys.

"There's the bird, Tessa!"

"Where?"

"Right there!" I said and stepped behind her, extending my arm along her cheek and pointing at the grouse now perched and motionless on the tree limb.

She raised her little 20-gauge Ithaca pump. BANG!

Low! She had shot underneath the bird. She didn't see it and was only shooting in the direction that I was pointing.

"No, no! Do you see the white and black bars?"

"Yes...no...maybe...the gun's stuck!"

If there is a god in this cover, I thought, let this bird sit just a little longer!

I took the gun from her and checked the action. She had short-stroked the slide in her excitement. I cleared the jam.

"Okay, here's the gun, safety is off, look at that tree with the black limb. Do you see it?"

"Yeah, yeah," her voice was starting to tremble.

Oh please don't cry, if you cry then I will cry and what a mess that will be.

"Just follow that limb with the barrel, the bird is right at the end of it."

BANG! It was still alive, and still sitting there. Then it moved.

"Oh gawd, I see it!" she said. "No shells, I'm out of shells!"

I only load two shells in my grouse guns and she had picked up this practice from watching me.

I reached over and plucked one out of her vest loop. "Here." I placed the yellow cartridge firmly in her hand. She never took her eyes off that partridge. I didn't either. Its light buff sides and dark bars are burned so deeply into my memory that I see it even today. It is suspended off the ground, waiting, patient and golden, to bring another child across that long bridge between impossible and possible.

BANG! "You got it!"

"Bravo, bravo!" I turned my head to the cheering and clapping. Spencer Turner, tank driver and Olympic athlete, was perched on the top of the log pile between his row and ours.

"That bird was born to be yours, Tessa," he said.

"I should have left it to pollute the gene pool with stupidity," I responded.

"It was the dogs. All the time you were fooling around, the dogs circled the tree. That grouse just sat up there and looked down at the dogs," Spence said.

Armor has another bad side effect. It is hard to hear in the windrows, and Turner is almost stone deaf.

We pushed on toward the alder swamp at the end, Tessa walking head down looking at the grouse in her hand, and me pushing the hairbrush-thick saplings out of our way.

A grouse flushed, and by its wing sound was headed across to Spence.

"Spence, bird's up!"

No response.

"Spence, your way!"

Same as before.

Crunch, crunch, crash, smash! The poplar whips shook and the berry bushes trembled over in his row.

In about another moment he would be on the spot that it settled into.

"SPENCE!"

Pause. "What?"

The bird flushed almost under his left foot.

He asked God's son for mercy...sort of.

I crawled up to the top of our common pile, placing my arms over the highest log and rested my chin in my hands. "Grouse," I replied.

He replied by saying that he was without fecal matter: "No ____!"

"We'll meet you at the log."

"Where's that?" he asked.

"Just follow any deer trail."

He didn't do that. He made his own trail. The dogs found the crossing with no trouble.

When he finally rumbled over to the log, both of his setters were well rested, my dogs were watered and happy, and Tessa had finally decided to put her grouse in her vest.

"Whew! Thick stuff! Where are we?"

I slowly relit my pipe. "Just downhill from the old homestead."

"No kidding! I love this place. I have almost a limit of woodcock, one grouse, and six productive points. I could stay here forever."

"Well, let's climb the hill and go back to the cars," I replied. "The next piece is easier to hunt, and if I leave you in there much longer I'll have to apply for a demolition permit."

The years have not dealt well with Turner's Windrow. It was messy to begin with and the current owner is not a farmer.

The big log piles have rotted down and the small trees are now large. Their shade has thinned down the great clumps of gray dogwood and the whole cover is headed into a recession.

I still hunt it, and when I am in there I can find the place where Tessa shot her first bird. And if I walk up slowly behind him, I can watch my friend Turner flattening the obstructions in front of him and steaming ever forward in pursuit of his white setters. He's slower than he used to be, and he talks himself through real heavy spots. I suspect that the bogey wheels of his corporeal tank are squeaking in an arthritic sort of way. But the driver inside there is just as enthusiastic as he was back when the woods were young and his best dog was still a pup.

Chapter 8
Whose Woods These Are

It is certainly true that in the forty-seven years of my existence every place that has created my past has changed and become part of other things. Even though my memory holds the past unaltered, I know that it is gone and will never come again. I can still see my father, in this place, walking the trail with my brother and me. The small pine corner where he stood, open mouthed, as five grouse rose up from behind a wet black log and disappeared into the rain is no longer there. I still see the beads of water on the gray receiver of his square-backed Remington automatic, his hat cocked to one side in the manner of every other hunter of his generation. Of all the coverts that I found, and hunted, none holds more afternoons of joy, cherished dead faces, and lost hours of my past than this one.

This is the woods on the other side of the homestead field. The cartway that runs past the door of the great old home splits here at the property corner. One branch travels past the ruins to the Pedersen farm, and we have followed that one to the end. This trail winds its way across the wooded valleys and tributaries flowing into the creek. In the South the dips would be called "draws" and the high ground would be crop fields. Here there are no crop fields, just "ridges." I never heard any name given to the low ground. The profit was in the trees. This trail was used by the loggers to skid the poplar and pine bolts to the log landing.

There are two of these landings in this forest. When I was a boy my father would drive our little Willys jeep along the trail while my brother and I pressed our noses against its Plexiglas windows searching the nearby brush for the quick scurry of a road-roosting grouse. As I said before, I was never very good at it and my attention would wander.

"Dad! What's that?"

The jeep jerked to a halt and my brother clawed at the door handle.

"Where is it?" my brother asked, pulling his Winchester pump out of its case.

"Where's what?" I answered.

"The partridge (you idiot)!"

"There's no partridge, I just wanted to know what that little building was next to the field."

"Ted," my father would warn (in his best judicial tone), "that's just an old cutter's shack. Now remember what we are doing out here and pay attention!"

The second landing had been opened up into a long field. The trail ran along one side, then cut over at the end to enter the woods again.

"Dad!"

The jeep didn't stop.

"What now?"

"What's that?"

"That's the bunkhouse and cook shack. It's a deer camp now and belongs to old Alfred," he answered.

"Let's stop!"

The radiator was bubbling over anyway—the old Willys heated up when she was forced along in low-crawl four-wheel drive. Dad got the tin pail out and walked over to the pitcher pump to get some cool water for the motor. Meanwhile, my brother kicked the back of the passenger seat. Every time the jeep stopped we got to switch places and he was in the mood to shoot something. I was high on his list.

"I think I'll look around," I said, and walked around the side of the building.

The walls and rafters were log. Tar paper was nailed on all sides and held in place by sawmill slabs. It had a peak roof, also tar paper, and a rusty stove pipe coming out one end of the cabin with a door on the opposite end. There was a barn-sash window next to the door and another in the stove-pipe wall. It was dark, exotic, and mysterious to an eleven-year-old. A game pole was nailed to one corner of the cabin, and along the crossbar there were rope creases pressed into the wood by the weight of hanging deer.

"Can I go in, Dad?"

"Go ahead, the door's open."

It pushed open with a wonderful creak, a perfect Tom Sawyer entry—there just had to be a pile of pirate treasure inside.

It was pretty Spartan. No treasure, just a crude table, two or three tired chairs, a set of bunk beds, and some up-ended blocks of wood for stools. In the corner was a big black cookstove with iron lids, and a few frying pans hanging on wall nails. The floor was rough-cut boards, and in the opposite corner stood a washstand with a basin under a long wooden kitchen shelf. The transition from the bright fall colors was profound and unsettling. It was as if the movie had suddenly turned from color to black-and-white. We had a coal bin in our home at that time and being in the cabin gave me that same feeling. It would be a great place to live if you were a spider.

"Let's go, boys!" called Dad. The Willys was cooled off and there were partridge to be murdered.

You won't find a whole lot written about road hunting. According to the outdoor press, grouse are to be taken over white setters on point in sunlit glades, among aspen leaves cascading down like gold coins. An outdoor cliché. In my boyhood, "partridge hunting" was done in the same vein as soldiers might forage for chickens. The bird was plentiful, the trails were driveable, and only a damn fool would work hard to get something that was able to be picked up at the side of a road. A deer was something to work for, something "worth shooting."

The first "sport" hunter I ever met was our neighbor's service buddy. He came from Oregon, an exotic location, with an honest-to-goodness hunting dog—a springer spaniel—and an honest-to-goodness bird gun, a Winchester Model 59 semi-auto with a lightweight fiberglass barrel. He had never hunted grouse before. He tried to encourage his companions; I overheard their chuckles after dinner.

"Old Ralph was walking after 'em today, yuk, yuk." The other one would answer: "Yeah, he was just shooting at shadows. Finally got him one on the road ditch." And so it went. He never came back. Which I thought was a pity, because the whole concept of a dog looking for a bird sounded interesting if not downright revolutionary.

Some of those sunny weekend afternoons would find as many as three cars following each other through the hills on the winding cartways. The passenger in each one had a cartridge in one hand and his gunstock in the other. Our old Willys had a door hook that we used to keep the back window shut. The loop on the end of the gun case would fit right around that hook and give a fast-draw advantage when the long shotgun had to come out of its case.

It was part of growing up, and one story was told by my father for as long as he was alive. He was driving his old black '49 Chevrolet. My brother and I were just little guys, maybe four and six years old. Dad spotted a partridge in the right-hand rut of the grass-centered trail. The car was stopped, he was out, gun loaded, and the bird shot in a space of time just about as long as it takes to read this. We jumped out, eager to be the first one to the bird. My brother won, and when he grabbed it by the leg it beat its wings in a flurry that sent both of us running back to the car as fast as we had tumbled out of it. How Dad would laugh when he told that story, his eyes brimming with tears.

That happened right in this piece of ground, for the trail was as well known among partridge road hunters as any interstate of today. The posting of land was uncommon. If the parcel was a woodlot, with no cattle in danger, everyone was welcome. A car passing through the woods on a Sunday afternoon during partridge season was assumed to be somebody local and not worth a casual glance. If the land was not worth farming it was not worth arguing about until deer season. I hunted this way all through my teen years, through college, and until I mustered out of the army. We didn't drive around all the time, my brother and I. Sometimes we would walk along the tote trails waiting for something to happen. A direct application of the theory trolling fisherman apply to big lakes: if you move around in one spot long enough you will bump into what you seek. Then I met Fred Corbett.

I have a photo of myself taken in the early fall of my first year back from Vietnam. My long old 12-gauge Remington Model 29 is in the crook of my left arm, resting on the sleeve of my camouflage jungle fatigues. Jungle booted and standing against the turning leaves of September, my only concession to bird hunting is the canvas cap that I have on my head. The same one I hung on the hook when I left for that hot, humid place over a year before. That was how Fred saw me, too. We met at the junction of two trails. He was coming out and I was having a sandwich. My dad's Willys was parked in his way, and after turning it around to clear the trail, I spoke with him about the grouse hunting.

Fred is from Florida, and right out of the pages of *Field & Stream*. Short and wiry, his face is tanned by fishing sun and weathered into grinning wrinkles. He carried a fine Ansley Fox shotgun on that day, grade AE, with marbled wood and silvery barrels. He wore a light-green hunting vest over butternut-colored clothes and spoke with an easy Southern drawl under a broad-brimmed hat. I spoke of this place and others like it. He must have seen something through the soldier suit, for we met again the next day in town and drove his old Ford Bronco out for a grouse hunt.

He was driving. I was directing the way. When we got to this trail I told him to turn left into the opening. He stopped.

"It's okay, Fred, drive on," I said.

"No, old pard, we'll walk 'em up." And we did.

I was foot hunting grouse for the first time in my life. We walked the trail a bit, turned off into places I now recognize as bird cover. We poked through the lush, wet edge of the creek and walked the edges of jack-pine groves.

A grouse flushed up on Fred's side and then, inexplicably, sat down on the trail edge. He didn't shoot. I assumed that he couldn't see it and blasted it in front of him and on his side.

"I hate to murder 'em," was all he said. To my credit, it was all he had to say.

Any man who could look at my Remington 29 and remark that it was a fine gun has proven his cloth is gentleman silk. I thought it was a fine gun then, but only until I handled his Fox. After that the double-gun bug took hold like a smallpox inoculation, and finer guns became the goal. I obtained a vest like Fred's and tried to imitate him in every way. My jungle fatigues became canvas trousers and light wool shirts. It is a good thing he went back south for the winter. I probably would have quit law school to enter the hardware business. He was retired from that, and from a sailboat that he and his friend took down the inland passage during the depression, a cattle ranch he almost bought in Arkansas, a quail paradise in Missouri, and a camp in the Florida Everglades. There is lots of time for talking when Fred hunts. "I don't talk slow, old pard, you just listen fast."

His knees gave out. He was bowlegged anyway, and the fact that he had stuck a camp ax in one didn't make them any more durable. When I am in the small draw that drains into the creek dogwood patch I can look back up to where it meets the grass field. He is still there, in golden butternut, packing his pipe and waiting for me to catch up.

This isn't a big place, only a hundred and twenty acres. I like to think of it as "compressed." A big place is five or six hundred acres, and we are going to move through a few of those in the following pages. Instead of size it has a depth of experiences. It has so many, in fact, that I had to subdivide its parts into covert names.

In order for my hunting companions to meet me in the right spot, I named the parking area the Trailer Site. An unhappy name. This is the corner where the trails split, and it was here that two children of nature put too much money down and bought the old house ruins and the little field that surrounded it. They arrived with a partial brood of kids, two goats, and a hoe to "live off the land." The woman who sold it to them was a client of mine, and I closed the deal (with my teeth clenched). She had two things to say when we talked about the pilgrims' welfare a few months later.

"They will find out that Mother Nature has a hard bosom." A better word-picture has seldom been painted. She added: "I don't know much about the woman, except that she has some fine copper dishes, and that man she married can pull a two-strand piece of barbwire farther than anyone I ever saw."

The neighbors were about as charitable. "He has a half-ton, four-wheel-drive truck with a three-speed transmission. Can you imagine that?"

My contribution to this analysis was silence. They had dragged an aluminum-sided trailer, turquoise and white, up on the hill, and the sewer was an open hole. Worst of all, the little pine thicket that was winter harbor to the corner covey got mowed down for no logical reason.

They were gone after a few years, froze out. But their refuse still remains, and thus the name Trailer Site.

When old Alfred, the owner of the deer shack, died, the land just stayed in his name until his nephew gathered enough family consents and made a purchase. I cleared the land title in exchange for a written lease that allowed what I hoped would be permanent bird hunting. Nothing changed in the cover for a couple years. Then I guess the nephew got the use of his father's diesel tractor and a bargain on fuel. The long second landing that had been golden grass with a brushy strip down the middle was converted by steel-disc plow to dry, dirty sand with the remains of a pretty good bird cover sticking out of the overturned sod.

After that I called the whole place the Disco, in memory of the thing that created it, as well as another pointless pastime.

So when I called a hunting partner and said that I would meet him at the Trailer Site and we would hunt the Disco, he knew exactly what I meant.

These woods were composed of far more than those two sad names. The First Field was uphill from the Creek Dogwoods, which ended at the Pines. From here I would hunt up the Happy Valley and cross over to the Shack Ruins. A shortcut through the hazel brush put me out to the Sand Field, and across from there was the Bee Sting. Finally the whole top side, on the north, was Norman's Field, and across that was an L-shaped parcel called Old Bob.

I said "was composed of far more" because the whole place is now in my past. It happened like this.

Every once in a while my back goes out. Sometimes it happens when I am working hard to lift something, but more often it seizes up when I reach for a fallen key or do something equally harmless. I was hunting the Creek Dogwoods. This is a place that has so much of a good thing along the creek that a hunter cannot stand upright and hunt it. The dogs get the birds moving along under the brushy limbs where the grass doesn't grow. This means I have to hustle along in a modified duck walk in hopes that one bird will stand long enough for a flush. If it does flush, the grouse will appear in a low window between the top of the dogwood bushes and the bottom of the poplar overstory. For the most part, however, it is a lot of bent-over walking.

My back locked up deep inside the cover. At first I was just annoyed and gimped to a log to rest. The muscle spasm did not go away. I tried a few steps and was rewarded with pain that can only be appreciated by those who have this affliction. The prospect of a long crawl through some rough country became very real. The little red gods that live in this place took mercy, and in a few minutes I recovered enough to limp out to the trail and back along it to the Shack Ruins, where my truck was parked.

I let the dogs inside the cab and poured some coffee. Sitting upright made me feel better, although I knew the day was over. Three new shiny pickups drove up—I could see them in the rear mirror. They waited for a minute, then the driver of one got out and walked up to my window. He was resplendent in a stiff new hunting vest with those bright orange pockets.

"Hi," he said, "you hunting here?"

"I was."

The pain in my back was foremost in my mind. This man was harmless to birds. If his vest had been in tatters, and his shirt hung with a dog whistle, I would have been worried. If the cab of his truck were soiled and two bird dogs were grinning out of the windows, one with a bandage on its ear, I would have been depressed on top of worried. But this guy was right out of the discount store. There was no logical reason to be short-tempered.

"Well I'm..." And he gave his name. "We talked to the owner and he said we could hunt this place."

My response was probably impatient if not abrupt: "I hold the lease, and I say you can't."

"Oh yeah, you must be Ted Lundrigan. The guy says you're the best bird hunter around here. This must be good too."

"I hunt it by myself and I like it that way." I could have lied and said it was no good. This fellow and those with him would be easy victims for the birds in the Happy Valley. But I had little tolerance for fools that day.

"Well, there's probably nothing left here to hunt anyway," he said. "We'll go across the road and hunt the state ground." With that said, the convoy drove off in a cloud of dust and spinning wheels.

Some people have a lot of money. I know that because I have separated a few of them from it. I learned, early on, that money and outward appearance are not indications of quality. About two months later the disc-plowing nephew called me.

"A guy wants to buy my land," he said. "He won't buy it unless you release your rights."

"How much is the offer?" I responded.

It was more than twice the going rate. The nephew wanted the money.

"I'll plow the whole works up if you don't help me," he said. He meant it; I had seen the proof.

"What's his name?" I asked.

He told me. It was the same harmless twit in the new vest. Maybe he couldn't harm my birds but he definitely gut-shot me.

I thought for a moment. "I don't want to see it torn up; pay me the fee I would have gotten ten years ago for the title work and you will have your release."

There is a sequel to this, an epilogue. The acquisitive nephew clear-cut the land right to the bone before turning over the ownership, and burned the old shack.

In the long run it will benefit the cover and in the short run it was something I thought of doing for revenge. I still look in on the place now and again, and I will be back when the new owner gets tired of the poor hunting it will offer for the next ten years or so.

In the meantime, I will tell you how it used to be.

Chapter 9
A Slide Inclination

I played trombone in the high school band. At least that was the excuse I gave the few snobs who inquired about my pump-action shotgun. My dad started the whole thing on my eleventh birthday. He didn't read enough outdoor literature. It was not his fault. As a lawyer, he spent a lot of his time with the written word. The last thing he wanted to do at home was read some more. He liked *Popular Mechanics*. His choice of my first gun showed it.

It was a used Remington Model 29 in 12-gauge with a full-choked 30-inch barrel. I was somewhat tall for my age, but that gun was as long as a pastor's sermon. He bought it from a noisy old gunsmith, who would, a couple years later, install a Lyman adjustable choke on the end of the barrel, thereby ruining any collector value the old clatterbox might have had. It had two things in its favor. It was a deluxe grade with a solid rib and it was so heavy that a hard swing would almost spin me around.

Among its other fine qualities, it could be defined in a word: complicated. We have to keep in mind that it was a bottom-ejecting and bottom-loading gun. A better one had already been invented by Remington in its fine Model 17. That design would be purchased by Ithaca, renamed as their Model 37, and go on its way into the slide-action hall of fame. But this one that I owned never could figure out how to get one job done and the other started.

I loved it like my first dog, and was completely unaware of its faults. With my Lyman choke at the end of that 30-inch barrel, I was the epitome of my dad's ideal: a One Gun Man. Never mind that my arms would ache on those few days when he and I and my brother would walk the trails. How I envied the way he could carry his square-backed automatic in the crook of his arm, cradling the back of the receiver with three fingers of his left hand. I had to stumble along behind with the full nine pounds of my long pumpgun pulling each arm. It was a stroke of lightning with a load of No. 6 shot on a road bird, but it took a jeep to haul it.

A law student is supposed to study for his bar examination during the six weeks between the end of his senior year and the date of the exam. I had that purpose in mind when I reserved a small study carrel in the stacks of the university library, but—as my father often pointed out—my attention wandered. I had lost some of my wonder at the intricacies of the law during my tour in Vietnam. I used my study breaks to browse through the literature shelves and came upon a volume written by Bob Nichols called *The Shotgunner*. It was a 1947 vintage book but I liked it a lot better than *Keeton on Torts*, and I suspect that I learned a lot more about shotguns than *res ipsa loquitor*. Things work out for the best, however, and I passed the bar and became acquainted with the Remington Model 31 at about the same time that the great state of Minnesota gave a

Vietnam veteran's cash bonus to each and every citizen who participated in the war to liberate the little people.

It was enough money to buy the pumpgun of my (and Bob Nichols') dreams: a used Model 31 Remington 12-gauge shotgun with the lightweight alloy receiver, the famous "ball-bearing slide action," and a 26-inch improved-cylinder barrel complete with ventilated rib. At six and one-half pounds it was lightning incarnate. I had already decided that neither civilization, nor law practice in the city had much to offer. I took my new shotgun and my new wife and returned to the woods.

I still have the shotgun and the woods.

I brought one other thing with me from my city years. After long and careful study in those same library stacks, I selected a hunting dog, ordered it, and picked it up at the airport before I moved back north. She was an American water spaniel. To her credit, she was well bred. To my dismay, she would not retrieve birds. I trained her by the book. She would do triple returns, blinds, take a line, stop on the whistle, sit, and change direction. Just as long as the object to retrieve was a canvas dummy. Otherwise, she hated birds. I remain grateful to her for the fact that she served as a bad example.

A black Labrador retriever wandered into our yard one day just at the perfect moment. I was trying to explain to my then-wife just what problems the water spaniel was causing.

"Here," I said, picking up a dummy, "this is how a dog is supposed to enter the water."

My wife had watched me standing in the water off the beach coaxing the spaniel to come out and get the dummy. I had never seen this black dog before that moment, but he had a good eager look about him, was young and strapping and interested in what I was doing.

I threw the dummy as hard as I could and before it hit the water the Labrador retriever was launched. He arched through the air, hitting the surface like a hydroplane. It was spectacular.

"That is how it's supposed to be done!" I declared.

The water spaniel yawned. My wife looked at the spaniel, then at the Lab, now swimming back with the dummy, and said, "Okay, so get one."

The dog who would become Dixie, my dear old black friend, did not arrive for another year. In the meantime half the team was proving up well. The Model 31 got a custom-fit stock in a straight-hand design and I got in the habit of loading two shells instead of three. It was so fast and smooth that I was wasting ammunition. I could empty the gun before the first smoking hull hit the ground. I usually missed with the first shot, killed with the second, and just shot the third into the leaves. These were not pointed birds. All that was yet to come. This was wild spaniel flushing, nerve-edge instinct shooting.

The water spaniel was killed by an unmarked trap. This can happen, especially if the hunting takes a man deep into the bush. Maybe a trapper decided the steel was not worth keeping or forgot it entirely. Perhaps it was a poacher's set. I don't know.

I forgot about that. My career was coming along well, I had lots of free time to hunt birds, and for the first time in my life I had a dog that knew its business. I trained Dixie, but I never had to show her what to do. All she needed to know was when I wanted it to happen.

I look back on it now: Fred Corbett's protégé, in canvas trousers, with a tattered shirt tucked in. I had my own sage-green vest, a faded orange cap and a lightweight, straight-stocked bird gun. There were some concessions to my own prejudices—the gun was a pump, the pants were tucked into my old jungle boots, and the bird dog was a Labrador retriever. If I saw that lean young man and his dog walking out of any of my coverts today, I would be worried.

And rightly so. In those years a lot of birds died. Quite a few were killed in the place I came to call the Disco. Eight hundred years from now, if someone digs up this piece of ground, they won't find a thing. There won't be a trace of the little pine grove that was a guaranteed morning roost for those birds in the first covey. The empty shell hulls will be long gone, just like my old car is in the junkyard now. But I was there, and so was my dog. We hunted alone and chased those birds down the ridges into the creek bottom. There was no corner or crevice of that land free from the tread of my jungle boots. I killed my fiftieth bird from that covey in the sun of an October's end. I was into numbers.

I don't apologize for that. We were good at our craft, Dixie and I, young and lean and hungry. That morning, numbers forty-eight and forty-nine had fallen almost consecutively. She had flushed them from under the pine thicket in a tight bunch. I was able to catch enough movement between the boughs and shot into an opening just ahead of a shadow. It was dark in the grove, backlit by the rising sun. It wasn't really a bird; it was a moving sound. Wherever it passed the light was blocked out, as it might be if you swung your hand in front of a wall of glowing windows. I didn't shoot at the bird; I just shot at the place where it was going to be. It was there when the shot arrived.

I didn't even look to see if I had hit it. I slipped the action open, shut it, and shot at another. I knew that if it was down Dixie would get it. I missed on the second shot; Dixie only brought back one bird.

We followed this group down the hill into the Creek Dogwoods. One of them held back, or landed early. It let me walk too close. I had learned to stop, and the pause unnerved the grouse. It flushed within a yard of my left foot, rising sharply above the undergrowth, then banking away in that classic calendar sweep all lit up by the early sun. I suppose my eyes and brain calculated the angle, sent the message to the trigger hand, lined up the gun barrel, and sent the shot. I don't remember even seeing the gun. All I saw was the bird flying and then falling.

"That's forty-nine, girl," I said as I took the grouse from her mouth. "If I can get one more it will be fifty!" As if the heavens would part on that number and a voice would ask me what I was going to do now that I had shot half a century of grouse.

I knew where I could get that one more. The rest of the covey was now scattered into the heavy cover along the creek, but there was a second and smaller group on the back side of the first field, between it and the long draw. They would be feeding just on the edge of the grass, soaking up some morning warmth.

We walked back through the pines up to the trail, then down it to the first landing. It was here that an old shack, much more primitive than the big one in the second field, used to be. Now it was just old black boards and tar paper. The rusted frame and fenders of a Model T Ford lay in a heap, once the proud power plant of a long-gone sawmill. About midway down the field, next to the trail, was a copse of bushes. Just one year ago a grouse had caught me relaxed and off guard as I walked back to my old car. It flushed out from under the bush and into the wide open, a flying circus wagon of noise and color. It got away untouched.

"Not this time" I promised myself, and crossed the opening.

A firewood cutter had dropped some trees along the field edge, fashioned a small dragging trail for the logs, taking the wood into the field, and then had bucked it up into chunks. Dixie followed this track into the cutting until she hit a fresh stream of scent. Her nose went down to the ground, leading her legs in a furious scuffle around, over, and through the debris. In a moment she was almost too far for my open-bored gun, and the bird jumped up in front of her by a good ten yards more.

It was a long shot, probably too far, but she was marking the grouse and I wanted it. The near wing snapped up at the shot like a broken green twig. I brought the gun down, opened the action, and pocketed the empty. It had been a bad shot, but good enough for Dixie. She brought the bird back. For such a historical item it was very unhappy. Clamped belly-up in the Lab's mouth, its head was raised and it glared like a stolen bride at a drunken wedding.

That year the hay in the second field had not been cut. I crossed through the draw and climbed its far side, coming out into the long edge where the trail was. The opening ran east and west. It had been a good year for grass; the crop was almost chest high. I remembered that my son had once made a small yarn square by weaving the material between the open spaces of two Popsicle sticks glued in the center and fashioned to look like a cross.

"This is the Eye of God," he said with five-year-old solemnity.

"I'll keep it forever," I answered and put it in the glove compartment of my old car, a decrepit Toyota station wagon nicknamed the Kamikaze (it was one of those vehicles that needed all the help it could get).

I loved that image, "the Eye of God," and the sky that mid-morning in October was so blue and cloudless that it was possible to see as far as heaven. If the sky was the Eye of God, then I could lie back in the tall yellow grass, spread my arms and legs out wide, and be a great warm fallen angel.

Fifty percent is considered pretty good odds. Most trial attorneys will take it; any card player would put money down if that was the chance on his next card. It is also the probability that any marriage will fail. Half the readers of this book know I am right, and that half has spent as much time in the woods as I have, wondering why.

The court part of it was over in mid-October.

During those years I enjoyed the companionship of other hunters. Among this diverse group was a dentist from Mason City, Iowa, Jerome Biebesheimer, and his good friend, a doctor, John Baker. I met these two men through the Ruffed Grouse Society publication, which was at that time a newspaper. I had written a letter to the editor inquiring whether anyone else had an interest in lightweight pumpguns. Jerome responded with a personal letter. He had an interest, if not a compulsion, in lightweight shotguns in general. He also hunted grouse very close to my small town. We made plans to meet.

In my region, a six-foot-tall man is about average. Jerome and John were both taller than that by half a foot. They were large in all aspects of humanity, taking their bites of life in huge gulps of good humor. These were pointing-dog men, but John, in particular, possessed enough tolerance for them both. His English setters were calendar specimens for the maxim, "If I can't do good, then I can look good!"

Years later John would fall in the parking lot of an opera theater, smashing his head on the pavement. He lost his sense of smell permanently. After I knew that he was otherwise recovered I pointed out that I had invited him and Jerome to hunt birds that weekend. To which he responded that he could now declare to his wife that his hearing selectively excluded opera, and that it was time for bird hunting.

After the accident John came up, on occasion, with his wife, who would stay in the car reading a book while John and I hunted. One of his setters once rolled in a brown greasy substance that it found next to the trail. It wasn't axle grease— at least it didn't smell like it, and very few mechanics work on axles in the woods and clean up with toilet tissue.

We had a grand time, and the dog did look good. We finished with a fast walk back to the cars, and John, in his usual load-and-go fashion, opened the back gate, boxed the dog in its crate, and got in the car.

"Good-bye, Ted, thanks for everything!" he boomed.

"John," came a small plaintive voice from the front of the car, "the dog stinks, did he get into something?"

"How the hell should I know?" he roared back. "I can't smell a damn thing. Har, har, har!"

It was going to be a long drive back to Mason City.

Jerome owned a small Brittany spaniel, which he ruled with an iron voice. She thought he hung the moon. If his coat pocket had been just a bit bigger he could have kept her in it, but she wouldn't have stayed. When the little spaniel came back with a grouse in her mouth one wing covered her head and the other dragged on the ground. She was thirty pounds of pure heart. Jerome's great height gave him the advantage of being able to see his little servant on point in tall places. He was called "Deadeye" by John in memory of five quail flushed and five dead in the air. I didn't call him anything other than a good friend.

Those were hard times for me, and it must have showed, for Jerome and John took me out to dinner. With a little pressing on their part I unloaded my soul. There was a pause after the confession, and then Jerome spoke. Whenever he talked, Jerome's words came out in bits and pieces with small, almost imperceptible pauses in between, as if his mind worked so fast that the thoughts had to line up to get out.

"We, ah, Presbyterians believe, that, ah, things work out, ah, for the best."

He was right. Even John's dogs helped as only they could.

The three of us were hunting in that part of a small creek tributary where it bends around the tall pine hill forming the end of the Creek Dogwoods covert. This small rivulet runs below the big golden grass field and over the eons had formed a valley. The sun had not yet risen to the treetops and the pines were cool and dark. So, also, was that little valley. Both places were as black as my mood. I was waiting for my two friends to finish their circle and come to the end of the field. As I stood in the trail I watched the creek water flow over the small dark pebbles. A quiet stillness came over me and I sensed a voice say, "Look up."

The woods formed an archway over the trail and there, in the middle of the arch, sunlit by the golden field grass were both of John's white setters. Robert Abbett could paint that sight, but not the feelings it evoked. No matter what else life could throw my way, I could be here to see these things. Some men can play golf better than others, some tennis—every man seems to have his niche. This was mine, hunting birds. As long as I could do it I would be all right. There is at least a 50 percent chance that you feel it, too.

Chapter 10

Remember Me This Way

She said it was time to make a will. "My husband is gone, we had no kids, and someone has to bury me." I told her what was required and we completed the task, setting out which assets went to each heir, and assigning one of them as her executor. "Who tells the undertaker what to do?" she asked.

"It's usually the person who looks after your business," I responded.

"Well, there's only me, so now it's you," she said, and handed me a brown manila envelope. "It's all there, and I expect you to see to it."

She stood, and with the direct manner of the woman who had raised and gambled fighting cocks for a living, walked out of my office, slender and straight.

Sometimes people can be too tough. She would not go quietly into that dark night. Mother Nature, with Her hard bosom, took her down piece by piece. When the end came I opened the envelope. I have often had that experience before, sorting through the papers of clients, but this time it was different. There was only one item, a show bill, and a note which said: "Closed casket, this on top."

It was a photo, enlarged and mounted on cardboard, with a place on the top for the name of a theater and the short, printed title underneath, "The Prettiest Stripper in Chicago."

She was a beauty, by the standards of any generation. Every sensual feature in perfect proportion to the next, a young vibrant woman in glorious display. A firm hand had written on it in blue ink in an upslanting script, "Remember me this way."

I took it to a frame shop and had the picture mounted and sealed in an ornate metal frame, placing it on top of her closed casket as instructed. When the service was over, I disobeyed her, but only momentarily: I opened the coffin and slid the picture inside.

Yesterday I was reading the morning paper. A reporter was complaining, in print, that people today don't want to know the whole picture. They just want "sound bites." The details of the big, important issues are being lost in the ten-second response that is remembered longer than a deep analysis. Maybe. But on the other hand, memory is sound bites. A bright, sharp, detailed picture is worth the proverbial thousand words. Any memory-improving course teaches us that we remember best by association. If you want to think of a name or an address or even a long subject, link it to a picture in your mind and it is frozen there for keeps.

The Pines, Creek Dogwoods, Happy Valley, the Sand Field, Bee Sting, and Shack Ruins are all gone, but I remember them this way.

We have all had this experience hunting grouse. A bird, wild flushed, comes right at our head and zooms over the top. "Wow!" we say. "I could have hit that one with my gun." Which to me is like the old story about the guy who was asked if he believed in baptism. "Believe in it?" he responded. "Hell, yes, I've seen it done!"

It happened on a sunny afternoon in the Pines covert. Spence Turner, my pear-shaped trout-biologist friend, was walking in the middle as three of us went down a small trail, single file, on our way back to the cars. I was at the end of the line. The dogs, tired from their work in the woods, were either goofing off up front, or scuffling around on one side or the other. Spence was carrying his Winchester 101 balanced on his right shoulder, trigger up, in the fashion of good quail hunters everywhere. The little trail runs along the top of a steep-sided ridge. One of the dogs, probably old Dixie, flushed a grouse from the brushy bottom.

I can see it coming even today as clearly as I saw it then. It flew hard and straight, rising as it climbed the steep side. Spence heard it coming, and half-turned toward the sound, bringing his shotgun up and forward into his other hand. Just at the moment the bird crested the top it was exactly in Spence's face.

He cut downward with the barrels and the bird struck them with a firm, metallic clink! It spun Spence around, completing the circle that he started, and knocked the grouse to the ground. They were both stunned for about a heartbeat. Then the bird, digging at the leaves with its feet, regained its senses and jumped back into the air. Spence shot it, as if he had intended it to happen exactly that way.

"The immaculate connection," I crowed. "I always said that gun was a club!"

"Can you believe that?" he wondered out loud.

Hell, yes, I thought, *I've seen it done.*

The dogwood cover was not manmade. The beaver had dammed up Wood Row Creek in several places in addition to the big pond at the Pederson farm. They gathered their construction wood from the trees on the side of the brook.

The opening that was created became a long dense thicket of gray dogwood bushes. The little gray-green berry is attached to heavy red-stem clusters on a bush that is about four feet high. These plants love the sun, and fill the area they inhabit so densely that all other growth is shaded out. Imagine a miniature park. The trees are fully leaved in red, the trunks closely spaced and bent. The ground underneath is covered with a short yellow grass. It would be a lovely place to have a picnic, if you were a leprechaun.

Now add a few sharp-pointed stumps to the grounds, and an occasional log that the beaver couldn't get down to the water, and you have the Creek Dogwoods. A place made for grouse, loved by them, and designed to frustrate bird hunters.

Dixie was a flushing dog and nothing could be done to change that. At first I hunted the Creek Dogwoods alone, starting at one end and pushing through to the other in the hope of killing a bird that flew back against the flush or curved away close enough for a chance. This was an ambitious tactic, but not a bright one. Later I would station myself about midway and on the highest point I could find. Then, having ordered Dixie to stay at one end, I would blow my whistle to release her. She would boil through the clear understory putting the birds up. I had a lot of fun, and some real sporting shots, but most of the covey would fly across the creek. This was especially true as the season ran along and they became accustomed to my method.

Salty made all the difference. She could stop them. All I had to do was wade in for the shot. I used a wonderful bronze bell with a clear musical tone to mark her progress. She would press through the thicket and I would walk along the outside, with Dixie at heel. When things got quiet, Dixie and I would creep through the bushes pushing aside the stems until we could see her tightened up on point. In a few more steps, and with a little luck, the bird would come up through the leaves and show itself for a moment above the tangle. This plan worked about as well as shooting a rifle from horseback. Like the old guide said, it can be done—once; after the first shot, all hell breaks loose. The same was true here. The dogs, both of them, ran after the other birds, and there was just no way to put it all together again.

The best way to hunt was to go in with two or three shooters and work it with one man in deep. The poor soul in deep might catch a glimpse of a bird, maybe even the flash of a tail, but his chances for a shot were slim. We used to trade off on this job, or if the opportunity came up, pass the work on to an unsuspecting volunteer.

Good things come in pairs. If you doubt that for a moment just look at fine shotguns, or the human anatomy. About the time Salty came into my life I lucked into a second hunting partner, Bill Habein. I needed a wood-burning stove and I admired one in the shop of an acquaintance. This fellow gave me Bill's name and address—or location, because there is no street address for where he lives. Upscale catalog buyers would get gushy if they saw his shop nestled in the woods, all painted in faded red siding and oozing that country charm which sells plaid shirts and woolly accessories. Bill is no phony; he's the real thing and lives in a log house made with his own hands. He is a blacksmith, forming iron and steel into items of strength and simplicity. On the one hand he is a complex man, seeking new thoughts, reading ideas, and deepening his almost limitless appreciation for all things fine and well made. On the other hand, he is German. This provides him with two more characteristics, a firm foundation in his own opinions and a limitless tolerance for me.

When it comes to plain damn fool antics he has seen it all. I once was so upset at a wild-flushed grouse that I insisted on thrashing through a piece of ground so thickly vandalized by a logging operation that a man could not walk on the ground. The only way through it was by hopping from one fallen tree trunk to another. After about two hundred yards of this he called to me from the fenceline, where he had stayed.

"I think I'll sit down and smoke my pipe. Both your dogs are over here anyway."

He was right, of course, and I quit following that small bit of Irish emotion in me that was insisting that sheer effort in a fruitless direction will gain results. I yielded to my Norwegian majority, which said, "Yah, dat seems about right."

"So wise a counselor and guide, so mighty a defender," goes a verse in some Lutheran hymnal. That is Bill. He would never say that. He doesn't collect sound bites and bits and snatches of life like I do. A life spent forming steel focuses the attention on durable things. Somewhere along the line he acquired a W. & C. Scott double, which he has effectively worn out, and now he shoots one or another of a pair of Beretta over-unders.

He is a fine woolly friend, bearded, and bound to the grouse, but not likely to be fooled into doing the inside edge of the Creek Dogwoods. He would do his share if it was his turn. Either one of us would give it up to a volunteer. We had one, but like the rifle shot off a horse, only one time. It was Bill's son, Luke, a biddable young recruit.

I don't remember who said it first, but I can tell you that the idea came almost simultaneously to us both. This was not unusual. We often went different directions in a dense cover and without a word spoken would turn up in the same place.

"You go down there next to the creek and walk along through the dogwoods. We'll be up here. Take your time, we'll wait." It must have been a sight to see two grown men grinning at each other so broadly as the whippy young sprout worked his way down the side hill, eager to be useful.

"Don't shoot unless you get a clear target," I called after him.

"Oh, you're a wicked, wicked man," Bill chuckled.

"Desperate times require desperate measures; do you think he'll catch on?"

"I hope not," Bill replied. "We could do this for weeks."

The birds were in there that morning. I couldn't see the boy but I could mark his progress as easily as I could hear Salty's bell. The brush crunched and the tops swayed as he pushed through trying to keep pace with the dog. Then there would be a short silence.

"Point!" he would yell.

Almost immediately after his yell, a grouse or two would flush out with a whir of wings. We would shoot and call for a dog or shout our encouragement to press on.

"Good boy! Keep at it!" punctuated by shots and instructions to "keep close to the creek." It was heavy going; twice I heard him struggle to shoot a rising bird, hanging his chance up in the dense branches. "Damn gun, stupid bush!"

We were doing very well. Bill and I each had two birds and Salty seemed positively inspired to find more of them now that she had a mole to follow her through the tunnels. The enthusiasm of youth was now properly harnessed.

"It's been kind of quiet," Bill said, "do you think he's caught on?"

"Naw, that last piece takes a real push; he's just out of breath. Hey Luke! Where are you?"

Silence, except for the single note of Salty's bell and the steady pant of Dixie's breathing.

"Luke!" Bill said. "Sound off, where are you?"

"Woof, woof," Luke answered.

"Yeah," I said, "he caught on."

If it was just a question of killing birds, my pumpgun would have been fine. It wasn't that snob thing either. In this area someone who hunts grouse as avidly as I do is not considered elite, just a little eccentric. No, I started using side-by-side double guns because I liked them. Bill and I did quite a lot of clay-bird shooting in the off-season. We wore out his Trius trap thrower and then, following a picture, made a better and faster thrower from the handle of a broken golf club. I used his W. & C. Scott and learned the touch and feel of a truly fine gun.

The best way to explain this is to hold the front leg of a big, tough Labrador retriever. Feel the muscles and sinew, the heavy, durable coat? That is a pumpgun—serviceable, hardy, and strong. Then pick up the leg of an English setter or a pointer. It is slender, lean, thin coated, and each time you move it the muscles slide over one another under your touch. That is a fine double gun. The difference is such as between a pickup and a sportscar. Both will provide transportation.

The first double gun I bought was an L. C. Smith 12-gauge, in grade 4E. I saw it on the store rack, handled it, coveted it, and traded away some money, two deer rifles, and another shotgun (not a Model 31) to get it. It was old, circa 1910, and beautiful, with engraved sidelocks and a long straight-gripped stock of fantastic Bastogne walnut. It had more drop than the Grand Canyon, but I could shoot such a gun. It was my sunshine girl. My fair-weather friend. I carried it often in the Disco and occasionally it misused me very badly.

That is the problem with fine doubles. Like sportscars they sometimes leave spots on the garage floor and won't start for any explainable reason. You have them because you love them. In this case the L. C. Smith had a three-position safety.

On-safe was in the middle. Off-safe was either pushed all the way forward, or all the way back. Can you imagine? A shotgun with reverse! Sometimes I got confused, especially after a hot run through the Creek Dogwoods. The safety would be all the way back, in the off position. (A safety will never prevent a hunting accident; only pointing the gun in a safe direction will do that, and there is no problem here.)

Bill and I had treed three grouse in a cluster of jack pine at the end of the dogwood cover and next to the trail. I saw one about halfway up, perched in the open on a bough. In a jack-pine grove this is a rare event. After a hard and empty run through a cover as thick and splintery as the Creek Dogwoods, a perched bird is a reward and vindication for effort expended. There it sat, peering stupidly down at Salty and Dixie, clearly a disgrace to its gene pool.

I backed away until I had a clear shot to the right, left, and straight overhead. Then I slid the safety forward, to the middle position, which in L. C. Smithese means "on." I probably even chuckled a little as I pointed the bird out to Bill and he picked up a stick.

"All set?" he asked.

"Never better," I responded.

The stick arched up and scored a perfect touch—not too hard, not too close—just enough to push the bird off its perch.

It did the usual down slip. I let that pass, then it straightened out and gave me a perfect right-to-left, belly-exposed flight line. It was going to die and this was going to be a wonderful memory.

"Umpth!" The muzzles jerked downward and the trigger did not budge. I slipped to the back trigger. "Unnnh." Same thing! The bird twisted over and banked left, then right again, and was gone.

I looked down at the gun. It had functioned perfectly. The safety proved to be worthy and the triggers were not bent up against the inside of the guard, although they should have been. I said some things then, but looking back at it now I suspect the way had been blazed before me by many previous owners of high-grade L. C. Smith shotguns and there really is nothing new under the sun.

The incident also proved an endless source of amusement for Bill, who reflected on it several times that day and many times afterward.

This exact spot in the Disco would later be featured in a story written by Mike McIntosh. It is on top of a hill. The trail turns here sharply to go downhill and across the little drainage that I spoke of before—the place where I was immersed in the stream and my own black thoughts of fate.

Mike lives for the trip, and that is why he, among those who hunt with me, loved this place more than all the other coverts. It was the ideal cover for those who consider the walk as important as the bird. The trails were always productive, and the way was scenic and unobstructed.

Mike has a thing for the 28-gauge. I could have used a more descriptive word, but I chose not to because the whole concept is about as involved as the walk-equals-the-bird theory. I don't subscribe to the gauge or the theory, but that never has gotten between us. I think that my predatory instincts serve as much as an amusement for him as my antics do for Bill. We are just different critters. Mike likes to walk with his gun balanced comfortably in the crook of an elbow, pipe lit, and hands pocketed. I hunt in the brush, both hands on the gun and eyes narrowed.

He was alone that day when he came to this curve. His Brittany spaniel, Toby, often maligned by me but utterly devoted to him, scuffled off into the jack pines and presently roused two grouse. These must have been noisy birds, for it was a quiet and cloudy day with a mist in the air. The first came out of the furry green wall and banked sharply to the right, carrying itself straight down the trail and swooping toward the creek crossing. Mike had been able to find some shells for the little gun in our local hardware store. He was disappointed because the box was high-base No. 6 shot. Now, however, that worked to his advantage and the heavy shot dropped the bird, dead, on the trail, almost halfway to the rivulet.

That pleased him. To prove it, he killed the second one coming straight in and it landed behind him. His dog got them both. I wasn't there, but he had the birds to prove it and I believed him. He could describe the moment so clearly, and in that place it could not have happened any other way. You see, there is magic in there when the clouds come down to earth.

Foggy woods are simply that—singular, monolithic, a chunk of obscured real estate. Foggy woods with a trail in them? This is something quite different. It is an invitation to push on. The trail divides at the golden grass field. One branch turns up to travel along the woods to the big shack. The other cuts along the base towards a small tongue of trees and through that to the Sand Field.

No place was more aptly named. The gopher mounds in that opening are sand dunes. Even the White Weed, able to grow on billiard balls, is sparse in this place. At the bottom of the field, to the south, is the Wood Row Creek drainage, still supporting good bird cover and running to the county road on the east. That direction would be to the right, and along this side of the field the woods are lowland brush and tamarack because the drainage broadens out and floods the land between here and the road. On the left, to the west, is the tongue of woods that carries up to the shack. At the north end, straight ahead, is Norman's Field, separated from the Sand Field by a fringe of poplar saplings.

This place, where I am standing, has an old hay rake buried in the corner by the road edge; a horse-drawn implement, judging from the wooden tongue and single tree. Every time I stand here I see two pictures. The first is of my brother and me, teenagers, looking up into the sky on a cloudy, misty, and magic late afternoon. The second is a careening, rolling, running, and reckless young setter that was my Salty.

When my brother and I were young hunters the Canada goose was rare. Waterfowlers who were lucky enough to get one had their picture on the front page of the local paper. We had been walking the trail, trolling our luck for grouse.

There had been no takers. It was a wet late afternoon with no wind and a lowering, misty sky. We stepped out into the corner of the Sand Field.

"I hear geese!" my brother said.

I could hear them too, coming toward us from the far end of the field.

"There they are!"

Yelping and clamoring, the geese strained to climb high over our heads. They may have been sitting at the far end, or perhaps we just happened to walk out at the moment when they were passing over. But no matter, for there they were, holding the promise of a kid's permanent fame among his peers.

We shot our guns empty and watched them fly away.

It never happened again. It didn't have to. We never forgot it. I came to that place with my brother and with others over the next several years and I could put my feet within inches of where I stood then and point up to the exact spot in the sky. I always thought the old brass and paper hulls could be found. Sort of like the ancient hay rake. I figured they would endure as a monument to past effort. But I guess like the hay that wasn't gathered and the geese that didn't fall, the memory lasts the longest.

It was right here that Salty fell over a grouse. It wasn't a dead one; it was alive and one of several feeding on the clover in the road opening. Salty had come on a flat-out charge, streaking up the brushy edge, running ahead of her nose for the joy of speed. I had come from the far end, walking across the field thinking of the covers ahead.

The bird must have been as distracted as I was, or perhaps it was very young and reluctant to fly. It crouched down, and when she hit it, both the bird and the dog rolled over. Salty skidded along her side, looking backward at the grouse with as close to a startled expression as a dog can muster. The bird regained its feet first, took two or three quick steps, and jumped into the air. Salty launched herself into the air after it, and flushed four more. She stopped, dumbstruck, like me, then dove into the underbrush, putting up two more.

I ran toward the field corner blowing my whistle and yelling. It was useless. She circled around and around through the nearby bushes and didn't return until Bill came up on the opposite side to see what all the commotion was about.

He was just about to ask me to explain when she ran up and fell over on her side, panting and gasping for air. I could not form words.

What a sight we must have made. I was gesturing at the road and the woods and foaming at the mouth. She was prostrate on the ground with her tongue lolling out and this huge canine grin that said, "Kill me boss, it's all worth it."

As I said, I have served as a source of endless amusement.

The joke has not always been on me. The Bee Sting covert got its name on the day that Spence Turner found the only living hornet in northern Minnesota. This place is the tree-line along the far right of the Sand Field, the part lying between the field and the floodplain of the creek. He was forging through the heavy growth in his usual tanklike fashion when he stopped, threw his cap on the ground, and turned around and around in small circles as if one of his tracks got locked up.

"Ow, ow, ow, damn, I just got stung!" he howled.

"What? What happened?" I asked.

"A bee, there's a bee in my cap!"

"Spence," I explained patiently, "this is October. There was a hard freeze last night. You could not have been stung." And I picked up his cap.

"Like hell." He rubbed the side of his head. "I've been stung before and I've just been stung now!"

I turned the cap inside out, and, sure enough, a yellow jacket was crawling around the hatband.

"Well, leave it to you to find a frozen bee that can still bite."

Bill and Luke were on the far right, and as I walked over to bring them up-to-date on the latest addition to Turner lore, a grouse flushed in front of Luke, who shot twice; passed in front of Bill who fired twice more, and zoomed past me. The bee sting incident helps me remember the place, and it is a less egotistical name than Wiped Yer Eye, which is what I did with one fast-swinging shot. Bill pointed out to me that I had the benefit of two bad examples, which ought to be enough for even a mediocre shot such as myself.

My response then is the same as it is now, a big grin and a slow nod.

I learned to do that early. You see, I killed my first bird on the wing in this covert. I did it with that great heavy cannon of a Model 29, all by myself.

My brother and I had split up. He was walking the grassy middle field up to the shack. I agreed to meet him there after walking along the edge of the Sand Field, taking a left at the top of the property line, and then hunting the woods edge where it bordered Norman's field. We had no dogs, just energy and youth.

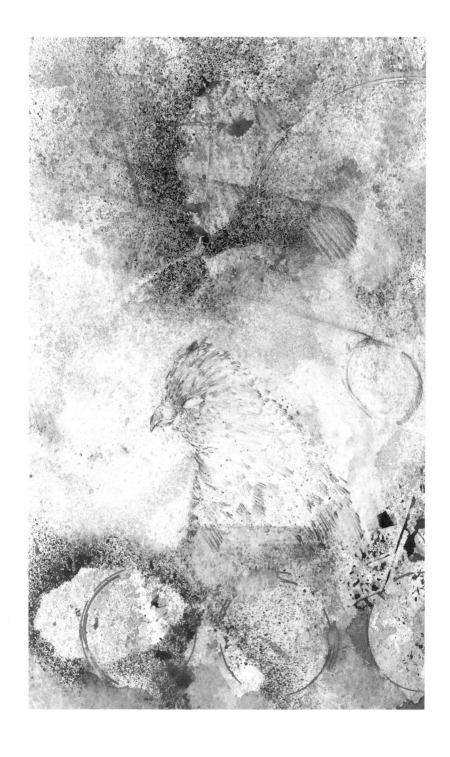

Chapter 11

The Magic Gun

Be careful what you wish for, you just might get it. That must have been written by a Norwegian sage. After all, this is the culture that brought us lutefisk. It probably started out innocently enough, most likely on a long voyage of adventure and piracy.

"Yah sure, Lars, I vish vee had some nice cod fish."

"You betcha, mebbe I vill ask my brutter-in-law, Iver, to figure it out."

So the inspired inventor threw fresh cod into a vat of lye for five days and, "uff dah," there it was: Fish Forever.

I have it on good authority that the only Norwegians who eat this are those who emigrated. It makes sense; it's not something that should be prepared on or near land. The Norwegians who stayed in the motherland probably said, "Clean up this mess and get the hell out of here!"

I once wished for a gun. The kind that never missed. I wanted one as lethal as the mythological cockatrice. A beast with a rooster's head and a serpent's body, hatched from a cock's egg, with an eye so lethal it could kill with a glance. A gun that quick would follow my eye and hands without a conscious thought on my part. Something like one of those automatic cameras that people call no-brainers.

I thought I had it with my lightweight Model 31 Remington. But a lot of the birds brought back by Dixie were still alive. The L. C. Smith was lovely to look at, and I once killed a double with it. However, it edged a lot of grouse wings. I wanted a bird that was limp, stone dead, one that fell from the air with a puff of feathers and a thump on the ground.

I bought a Fox 12-gauge. It had a nice straight-hand grip, but with trigger pulls at about twelve pounds each the gun was not what one could call "instinctive." I bought a fast and whippy AyA 20-gauge. It carried very nicely at less than five and a half pounds, but I can still see a big red-tailed grouse rising from my left, lifting up and over the brush, turning its belly toward me, and flying away completely untouched. I bought a Browning Superposed 20-gauge with a Belgian pedigree. It had a wrist as slim as a chorus girl's ankle. If I had wanted to commit suicide with it I would have needed two shells. No, I am not like a lot of guys who wish for the return of a long-gone gun. I left those without regret.

The gun I was looking for is familiar to all target shooters. It is the "magic gun." Any trap or skeet man knows this piece. When the slump comes, the magic gun is the one that they pick up from the rack with the prelude of, "Hey, can I try your gun?"

The shooter's nerve endings wake up, his eye is regained, his subconscious is stirred to pay attention because something is different. He promptly runs twenty-five straight, does it again, and the deal is made. After a week or two, the magic wears off. The shooter finds out it was not the gun; it was, as usual, the nut behind the barrel.

The target game is different from bird shooting. The target location, speed, and distance—everything but the gunner— is controlled. That is not to say it is easy. It is just different. A shift in stance, aiming point, gunfit, or trigger pull can change everything. In grouse hunting, dumb luck, terrain, angle, speed, fatigue, and weather can change any of the previous factors at any time.

The gun I wanted had to kill with a glance. It had to be wielded without a conscious thought. I have attained a black-belt rank in Hokkoryu Karate Jitsu. Part of this discipline is based upon the art of Kendo, best described as Japanese swords-manship. The ultimate goal of its practitioners is to strike with the sword, and not be aware of it. There is a Japanese term for this level of performance which roughly translated means "the sword of no sword" and "to act without think-ing." I have not made it to the rank where swords are actu-ally passed out, but that is not for lack of practice. The strikes and blocks are repeated again and again as if the blade was part of the movement. The purpose of the training is to repeat the physical movement until the sword is irrelevant. If all this sounds a bit occult, you'll have to trust me when I say it works. I have been knocked unconscious twice, suffered dislocated fingers and a cut chin, without seeing a thing coming. I am glad we did not have swords.

There is a danger in physical performance at that level. A person should think about the fact that the edge of his foot or hand is going to strike another human being. Maybe it should not happen. A martial art technique, correctly executed, is lethal. Ignore the current rage of hop-and-chop movies. Only one strike is necessary. It is for this reason that the mental preparation is done independent of the physi-cal. The single most important element of all martial train-ing is the state of mind known as *cho*, or calm. Anger has no value. The purpose of the training is to bring a controlled presence to a chaotic situation. A gentle answer turns aside wrath, so the saying goes. To accomplish this purpose without endangering yourself, however, the body must react instantly to an attack.

I have that calm state of mind when I am bird hunting. The place is beautiful, I am doing what I enjoy, and, if I am not too tired or angry, I react instantly to the flush. If the gun does its part, killing with a glance, the circle is complete.

The magic gun is not mine. It belongs to Mike McIntosh. It is the duplicate of an English gun that Mike owns, built to the same specifications by AyA of Spain. The original, a Wilkes sidelock London "best," is a grand campaigner known as Old Bob. This is Mike's sunshine gun. The one he carries when he talks tweed coats and wine corks. He had the Spanish gun built as a traveling companion for rainy days, provincial companionship, and splintery grouse covers like the one where Old Bob got its name.

There is a grass pasture that stretches almost all the way from the old town road on the west to where Wood Row Creek meets the wooded edge of the Sand Field. Every place I have hunted before this moment is south of this pasture. I like to eat lunch here. The grass is short and green, and if the day is sunny the trees on its edge shade my folding chair. I can sit and look out to the north, to the east and west, and enjoy a breeze. I was seated when I found the Old Bob grouse covert by whimsy.

A deer was grazing in the pasture, content to crop the new-growth alfalfa and follow her nose around the cut rows. She would twitch her tail just before she raised her head to look at me. It was the same every time—stare at me, drop her head to eat, twitch her tail, lift up her head to stare again.

"How close can I can get?" I wondered out loud. She stared, looked ahead, and took a few steps toward the woods' edge. Looking down on us, a hawk would have seen the old Kamikaze parked on the top edge of the Disco-Sand Field covert.

On the deer's side of the pasture was a strip of regrowth poplar, tall, about fifteen to twenty years old, with a heavy border of dense brush and dogwood bushes. On the far end, to the east, was another strip of woods making the short leg of an L to the deer's side. On the other end was the town road. I had never been across the pasture to the woods. I had looked at it, but it just never seemed, well, birdy.

I stood up when the doe lowered her head to feed. As long as she kept her head down I would walk toward her. When her tail twitched, I would stop and would stand utterly still. I closed the distance between us to almost twenty feet before she started to stare at me a little longer. She was getting nervous. In a few more repetitions I was within an easy ten feet. She started to walk away, wanting to get nearer to the woods.

There was no wind, and the green alfalfa didn't crunch underfoot. A deer has black whiskers in that dark band of color around its nose. When it is quizzical about something the whiskers move up and down like little feelers. She stared more than she ate. I would not make eye contact with her; if I did that, I was certain she would realize that the walking tree was alive.

She turned around and faced me. Staring intently, she stamped her hoof. She stamped again. At that moment I looked her directly in the eye.

The effect was electric. She spun on her heels and in two leaps made the woods' edge. Her surprise was not over. As she cleared the brushy edge two grouse flushed up underneath her. I laughed at her next leap, which was twice as high as the others, and went back to get my shotgun.

The part across from the car was a rough piece of ground. The trees had been cut helter-skelter, some picked up and others left to rot. It was thick as a boar-bristle brush. The birds must have flown in a direction different from the one I was headed, so in the interest of exploration I turned the dogs toward the corner where my part met the segment coming from the Sand Field side. The trees were older and the game trails more numerous. It bordered a low wet backwater of the creek bottom. The dogs were apathetic about the whole place. The only significant feature was a deer trail from the corner of the field back into the interior.

We followed this, single file—Salty in the lead, Dixie next, and me bringing up the rear. It twisted down and around a hallway of poplar sprouts, then uphill where a two-strand fence of rusty barbwire stopped us. Looking down one side I saw more brush. But on the other side I saw enough gray dogwood berries to cut with a self-propelled combine. If little gray berries were gold I had found the mother lode. McIntosh was due the next day. I called the dogs in. We would wait until then.

"I have a new covert." I said.

Mike nodded his head, "Good, I have a new gun. It's an AyA made to be exactly like the Wilkes. I wanted something that I could shoot, ship ahead of me, or chance in airline luggage."

"Can I try it?" I asked.

"Absolutely, I haven't fired it at a bird. Carry it tomorrow; I want to use the Wilkes."

"Providing the sun shines," I interjected.

"That goes without saying," Mike answered, and handed me the fitted case.

It was a beauty. I was familiar with the feel of the Wilkes. This was tighter, bonier, with a long stock and a diamond-shaped grip. The gun was not the Wilkes, it was deadlier, an edged weapon. If the two guns were people, the Wilkes would be a colonial colonel, the AyA would be yon Cassius with a lean and hungry look.

The next morning was sunny, but we started late. Mike and I had stayed up with the Maker's Mark bourbon. I have a small log cabin on my place reserved for friends. It was built in the middle 1930s. The log walls and ceiling inside were lacquered annually until the last of its original owners left fifty years later. When the pipes are lit and the bourbon flows it is a wonderful place to be. Mike reviews his travels and recharges my fascination for the members of the "waxed cotton crowd."

To some extent, outdoor writers have a free ticket to hunt and fish with select companions and good guides the world over. Mike tells me that for the price of my kid's college education, shooters in Hungary can knock off three hundred pheasant in a day. In Central and South America the sport doesn't quit until it gets dark. My failure to attend these places is excusable. I can't afford it. Even if I could, I just like to do things my own way. And not for a lack of good manners. Courtesy is the same all over the world. I have enough confidence to make a good accounting of myself in any shooting game. I lack a worldwide reputation and a well-heeled publisher. Also, I have this streak of perversion: I am inclined to put my pumpgun in a rack of fine doubles.

I like to think of myself as Mike's touchstone to reality. Around this neighborhood he has to pack his own lunch, and carry his own birds. That day he carried away five grouse, a limit, and one other thing. I expected the five birds, for he is a fine shot. I did not expect the other thing, and I blame the magic gun, in part, for it.

There were two coveys of six birds each in the new covert, making a total of twelve grouse flushes in two hours. He killed four woodcock, which I don't shoot, and three of the grouse. I had one good opportunity and took advantage of it using my own gun. Salty did her part flawlessly, but in grouse hunting a flush, even off a point, is not necessarily a good opportunity. This is especially true in heavy gray dogwood covers, where the birds run under the canopy until they can find a spot to launch. Then if the bird is young it will rise only to the top of the brush and dip down again. These birds were from two family groups. My bird, and Mike's three, were all young of the year. We came back to the old car for lunch and a short nap.

"What do you call that place?" Mike asked.

"Doesn't have a name," I answered.

That held for a while. Mike was packing his pipe as I rummaged in the back among the guns. I had an inspiration.

"Whose initials are on the stock oval of your Wilkes?" I asked.

He gave a name, "Robert" something.

"Then with the powers vested in me I hereby dub your Wilkes, and that covert, Old Bob."

"Fair enough," Mike answered. "Where do we go next?"

I took his AyA out of its case and assembled it. The greatest Japanese sword maker in the world was Masamune. His blades were perfectly balanced, like this gun. They were assembled in seven separate layers, each of differing flexibility yet bound to one another in the perfect harmony of Soshiu Kitae. They could not have reflected the color, shape, and beauty of the master's skill better than this. This gun was a cockatrice. It would kill with a glance.

"Only one place for us, the Cookie Jar."

"That motion is made, seconded, and carried; let's go."

The Cookie Jar covert lies on the other side of Wood Row Creek. It was so named, by me, in commemoration of what it contained when I first found it. There were twenty-four separate birds in its five acres. This singular astounding event never happened again, but the covert was always good for fast action. It was reached on foot by walking along the Disco-Sand Field edge to the creek bank. Then we would dig out two old planks that I had stored in the brush and drop them across the flow. This primitive bridge spanned the deep part and we could hop from one hummock to another to regain the high ground.

The land between the high ground and the Cookie Jar held the remains of a hard-rock farm called the Mentor Place. To call it a farm would be charitable, because the two small fields that composed it were pried out of the soil many years ago. The home buildings were up near the road. Our direction would take us along the soft ground of the creek, upstream, parallel to the back side of the Disco, and returning toward the Creek Dogwoods and the Trailer Site.

I have shot grouse in the Mentor. It is like the Caterpillar covert, a transition from one good place to another. If the birds are to be found here they will be right on the edge of the sod-bound fields. Salty knows this and sweeps on ahead. Both Mike and I walk with long strides, putting the distance behind us, with our minds already in the covey that must be ahead.

I saw her tail first, then the long straight line of her back. She was pointing on the edge of the last field facing into a cluster of three dark green spruce trees.

"Point," I called out to Mike. He nodded, and with a gesture indicated that he would try to work in below the spruce. It was a tough spot. I was on the field side, so the bird would not break my way unless it was open. The brush below the pine trees offered no clear avenue. Even worse, the light was at my back, making the shadows around the point impenetrable.

I heard the flush—it was not even ten yards away—but I didn't have a glimpse. A soft voice filtered up to me through the underbrush. In that resigned tone reserved for talking to oneself, Mike said, "Well, I guess that's why they call it hunting."

We had to cross one more small stream (with a short jump), and the Cookie Jar was in front of us. Our plan was simple. I would work over to the side of the covert that was next to the cornfield and downwind from the creek. Mike would walk the creekside and the dogs would hunt between us.

I flushed the first on my own. It was on a perch about halfway between the ground and the treetops. The bird took a hard diving slant out and away from me. I glanced at it, and it was dead. Just like that, falling from a cloud of feathers.

"Helluva shot!" Mike yelled.

"Yes it was," I murmured, and looked down the long smooth barrels. The gun had killed its first bird with its first shot. I opened the action and caught the empty in my hand. Nothing unusual about the shell. It was the same load I always use, a Federal P162 (now discontinued, of course), with $3\frac{1}{4}$ dram of powder under $1\frac{1}{8}$ ounces of copper $7\frac{1}{2}$ shot. Dixie brought me the grouse. It was stone dead, limp, struck by lightning.

We pressed on. Salty pointed and then flushed a woodcock past Mike, who killed his fifth and retrieved it himself. A grouse flushed to his right, prompting two quick shots, which startled another bird, even closer, to rise up before hisempty gun and flutter away like a badminton shuttle.

A fallen pine blocked my way. As I stepped over the down end, Dixie hustled past me to flush a third grouse into high gear. It was a dark shadow clipping between tree trunks. There was only one small opening before it would be gone. I looked at that spot and the gun took over. The bird was knocked upside down, bounced off a tree, and fell into the leaves.

Two in a row. Dixie ran to get the retrieve, picked it up, and in turning to come back flushed yet another grouse straight at me. It was a no-brainer, all instinct, an in-your-face-and-dead shot. I could have caught it with my cap.

"That's three shots and three birds!" I said.

"I'd say my new gun is getting broke in right," Mike answered.

"I would say it is magic," and I was right—black magic.

The Cookie Jar is a one-way walk; it ends in a small wood-cock hole directly across the stream from the Creek Dogwoods. Walking farther ahead meets the field that runs along one side of Turner's Windrow, the same one overlooked by the old house ruins. Wood Row Creek blocks the low side. A quick swing through the doodle hole flushed the two or three that hang out there. Salty pointed woodcock; I just didn't care to shoot them, and Mike already had a limit.

Salty and I had an agreement. I would shoot at, near, or in the direction of every fifth one. If I failed to keep my end of the deal and just kicked them up into the air, she would pout. The next point would be busted and the bird pushed out. I suppose she just liked to receive credit for her work in the form of gunfire applause. She had no interest in dead birds—dead woodcock in particular. That was the retriever's job. But she kept track, and after a few discussions she and I settled on the number five.

Mike stood in the little clearing at the end of the Cookie Jar until Salty and I completed our wake-up circuit. Fortunately there were only two points, so the perfect record of the magic gun was unspoiled.

We now headed straight away from the creek and through a long strip of very dense blown-down hardwoods. This narrow piece of woods was more or less shaped like a right-angle triangle. The ninety-degree left-hand corner was where Mike was standing. About a half-mile ahead of him was the driest place on earth: Six Pack Corner. On his left was a cornfield. On his right were the stone piles from the field and the woods. His part of the hunt was to walk the edge, just the job for a guy who savors the trip. It would take a cocker spaniel with the heart of a lion to push through the debris that was on his side of the covert.

I would hunt the long side of the triangle, working in and out of the edge as it angled back toward Mike's side to meet at the top. This was a good plan. Mike walks slow, picking up an interesting rock, perhaps, or digging for matches to light his pipe. I hunt fast, pushing into good-looking corners, but generally paying attention to the dogs.

This day, however, Mike walked fast. He still would have been okay, except for one small detail. I had the Magic Gun.

Louis Nizer, a superb trial attorney, speculated in his book *The Implosion Conspiracy* that historical events are the haphazard collection of small unrelated circumstances that come together in unexpected ways.

I did not expect the grouse to flush at the very end of the covert, unpointed, on its own. Nor did I see it take off. Suddenly it was just there! The shot was impossible. The bird was in a small opening driving hard toward my left shoulder, coming in fast, and shortening the angle with every wingbeat. I moved, without a conscious thought. No, there was one thought: *Impossible*.

This gun *was* the cockatrice, the mythical, magical killer at a glance. But the impossible did not take nearly long enough. Another, heavier gun would have come up too slow and I would not have taken the shot. A lighter gun could not have caught up. The Magic Gun busted the grouse right before my eyes.

And Michael had walked too fast.

"That's unbelievable!" I crowed. "This gun is pure death!"

It seemed peculiar that Mike didn't answer. I walked across the leafy screen between us and saw him sitting in the field. He was cross-legged as if in meditation, and very quiet. His English gun was on the grass in front of him and he was staring with a profound fascination at the drops of blood falling from his right cheek into his open hand.

I walked over, got down on one knee, and put my hand on his back.

"Mike?"

"I'm shot," he answered.

He didn't scream it, howl in pain, or do anything other than contemplate those bright red drops.

My voice said, "Where?" My mind said, *Impossible!*

He looked up into my face. I could see a small, red, weeping hole just below his cheekbone.

"I see it, where else?" He pulled his shirt out from his chest. Two more 7½ pellets had penetrated his vest and shirt and had lodged under the skin there. He held his right hand out and showed me a cut on his little finger, which had also been hit.

I took my bandanna out of my hip pocket, folded it, and pressed it against his face. "Hold this tight for a minute."

I sat down next to him, opened the gun, and shook my head back and forth in denial. My brain said impossible. My eyes saw different.

I am not a stranger to gunshot wounds. I wish it were otherwise. I don't put on old jungle fatigues and weep at the black stone wall to rid myself of demons. A lot of unrelated circumstances beginning with the date of my birth put me in the country of Vietnam, and a few other peculiar events made me a medic. I dealt with all that my eyes saw over there by not letting my mind think about it. I developed a numbness where others feel horror. I stored it all in a small black corner of my brain, accessible only at 2:00 A.M.

I felt relief. Mike was going to be fine. At the same time I felt very sad. I was responsible for having put this force into motion.

I had wished for a gun that could kill with a glance. Another man had built a different gun thousands of miles away. A few more men had assembled a copy of it, but had made the replica greater than its model. Mike had brought the gun to me, and though built for him, it had blended with my metaphysical being in an unholy way. All those unrelated circumstances meshing in layers until, in the ultimate ironical twist, he was shot with it.

I can't minimize my part in this; guns don't kill unless they are pointed by man. Doesn't it say in the Old Testament book of Isaiah, "Shall the clay say to him that fashioneth it, 'What makest thou?'"

True enough, the tool is inanimate. But Picasso painted with the same brushes as his contemporaries, and a Stradivarius is just a violin until it is in the hands of Itzhak Perlman.

Does that mean I was the master gunner of all time? I don't know, and I'm not going to find out. He took the gun back home. I haven't asked to use it again and he hasn't offered.

Chapter 12
One Good Turn

Books on grouse habitat seldom mention cows. There is usually lots of talk about "dominant timber species" and "early successional stages," and even "parkland ecotone." Such books must be written by authors who manage public lands, boreal bureaucrats paid by the government to form the written bible for land policies. I own a copy of *The Ruffed Grouse: Life History, Propagation, and Management*, the three-inch-thick classic written by Gardiner Bump, et al. All of the really serious grouse hunters have this on their bookshelf. I also have a Bible.

I have a confession to make: I have not read either one very completely. I have read bits and parts, but not enough to be a minister of either religion. Neither volume gives much credit to cows. The grouse book is mostly concerned with the study of that single species and its life on public lands. No cows there. The Bible is mostly concerned with, well, biblical things.

If it hadn't been for a cow, however, I never would have found Uncle Willie's. Ultimately, the same critters did the covert in, but until then we had a helluva ride!

Every farm woodlot, besides yielding lumber, firewood, and fence posts, provides some pasture for livestock. This is certainly true here in my part of Minnesota where the soil is more rock than sand. Willie Weiss was born within a few miles of his farm. He married his neighbor's daughter, Marlys, and they bought and settled on the land north of the Pedersen farm, Wood Row Creek, the Disco, and all those other coverts. Willie was a carpenter during the day and a farmer every other waking hour. He raised a few head of cattle, some hay to feed them, and when the mood struck him he could put down some corn in his fields.

His farm straddled Goblin Creek. This little rivulet is a cold-water brook trout stream originating somewhere in the Spider Lake foothills. It winds its way east more or less parallel to the Wood Row Creek watershed, and then, after flowing through Willie's land, turns north through a ditch into the next farm, belonging to Frank and Walt Olson.

Willie didn't dig this ditch. Except for using it as a cattle crossing, he was content to leave the stream alone. The ditch was dug by another of Willie's neighbors to move the water course in an orderly fashion across that man's crop field. He wanted to move it out of the way of his tractor. The stream level was subject to the whims of the beaver anyway, and it made more sense to give it some direction. During those few times when there was enough water to make a small river, the land served only as transportation support. There were no trees and no fish.

The public powers that be, however, took alarm and cited the owner for his misdeed. They believed that it was an inviolable trout stream. Perhaps it was, about six miles upstream, but not in the middle of a cornfield. I got involved in my professional capacity as defender of the accused. The confrontation was short and the government lost. But the day after the decision, Walt Olson told me that the trout hatchery truck stopped on the county road and dumped a load of fingerlings into the ditch, thereby proving for future reference that there were, indeed, trout in the lower reaches of the Goblin.

But I digress; my subject was cows, not public management practices.

I was driving my old Kamikaze station wagon up the road, having finished a sunny afternoon hunting the Pedersen farm and environs. I passed Willie's farm buildings—neat, white, and orderly—and was rolling downhill to the culvert that spanned Goblin Creek. The land on Willie's side of the road was black spruce lowland with a hardwood mix of poplar, alder, a few oaks, and some ash trees. It was fenced along the right-of-way. Some cattle were grazing next to the road. The land between the buildings and the stream slanted downhill in open green spans of cropped lawn until it reached the edge of the alders and spruce. Then the area broke up into creek bottom, became the waterway of the stream, and climbed back up through dense brush and trees to the open fields ahead. Two head of young stock pushed through the fence, scrambled up the ditch bank, and stood in my way on the road.

I am not fond of cows. I hunted a cover not far from here that was terrorized by a cow with an ear tag numbered 13. She chased me and my dog across two old splintery windrows one morning with the pure malicious intent of rubbing us into grease. I was having coffee and reflecting on this singular event when the cattle owner joined me for a cup. He was clearly amused.

"Har, har, har," he yelped. "I know it." His brown weathered face was creased into a toothless grin. "That old bandit got my boy down in the cow yard this spring, rolled him over and over in the manure till the only white thing on him was his eyes. They was THIS BIG!"

I do know the value of young beef, however, so I turned around and drove back to the farm. Willie wouldn't want his livestock spread on the road by a hill-hopping tourist.

I enjoy Willie's driveway. It is always level and smooth. He pulls an ancient road-grading blade behind his tractor with Marlys at the controls. She rolls the earth just so, crowning the middle and blending the holes into the surface while he motors along listening for directions.

They had a brown farm dog that was official greeter and mooch. He was part something and mostly basset. He camped on the front step next to the metal boot scraper. A good ear scratching lasted just long enough to bring Willie to the door.

"Willie, a couple of your calves are out on the road; hop in and I'll take you down," I said.

"Oh, you don't have to do that, Ted," he drawled, "I'll get 'em myself." Which is Minnesotan for "Thanks, I'll get my hat and be right with you."

It didn't take long for the two of us to chase them back into the pasture. He told me they were both experienced fence jumpers. We leaned on the fenders of my old car and talked.

"What brings you out here today?" he asked.

Willie is a bright man; he saw my bird-shooting clothes and the dogs. He was working his way around to thanking me in the quiet way of country people.

"Bird hunting. I was down on the Pedersen place."

We had a long discussion about that family and the farm, and then he said: "You know, I scare up a fair number of partridge around here, you ought to try it. Can't shoot 'em myself, too fast, but one time I shot a Canada goose in the pasture..." and he finished the invitation with a story about a migrant flock of geese that settled into his farm south of the house.

"I'd like that very much, Willie," I answered, and Uncle Willie's grouse covert was born. He wasn't my uncle, you understand; I took the name a couple years later from a conversation I had with his nephew, who asked me if I was having any luck in "Uncle Willie's." I have a very small extended family, no uncles left alive. But if I had one, I would want him to be just like Willie Weiss.

It turned out that he was a master of understatement. I put up twenty-five grouse in three separate coveys. There was one group in the creek bottom. This was a corridor of spruce and poplar with alder thickets on both sides of the stream. The township road was where it ended. The water flowed underneath it and out into the dead trout ditch. The other side of the covert had a combination beaver dam and rusty wire fence for a boundary. The beaver dam was old and eroded down into a long twisted berm. The downstream side was a heavy poplar and alder growth. Upstream of this was an open-grass dry slough, being the dried-up bed of the reservoir. This part of Willie's pasture was where the earth narrowed before it flattened itself out to his neighbor's crop field across the road. It was a funnel of sorts, narrow at the road, broad at the slough, and high on both sides. He had made a little road right in the middle, dropping a culvert to run his machinery across. Most of the time the stream avoided the culvert, flowing freely on both sides. This made a fine dividing point to organize the place into two distinct hunting zones. The part between the crossing and the road was a meandering, creek-bank walk. It had tall yellow ash trees and dark brooding spruce groves. The part from the crossing to the slough was heavy alder, soft underfoot and lumpy with thick brush. It was so dense that I saw my brother fall and then hang suspended by the alders where he had tripped.

"Ted!" he hollered, "I'm hung up in the brush, there's a grouse right in front of me!"

I came running on the double, in time to observe him struggling manfully to right himself and bring his gun to bear on a bird that was, at the same time, trying unsuccessfully to leap up and out of the tangle. The grouse jumped up and fell down again and again. Then it gave up and ran off, leaving a cloud of floating feathers.

"Can you see it?" He looked over at me. "Can you stand up and stop laughing?"

There is a small hump just behind this very spot. It is a grassy knoll surrounded by spruce but open in the middle. The first day I came into the covert I flushed four grouse from the middle of it. They spread out like the spokes on a wheel. The best guide in a strange grouse cover is the bird itself. By avoiding predators for months, it knows exactly where it wants to be next. Two of these crossed the pasture fence flying uphill into the rest of Willie's woodlot.

It is right at this point that public land management policies and I part company. If the rest of the cover had been under book rules there would have been a wall of doghair poplar saplings eight to ten feet high right in my face. In government theory those two grouse would have been huntable, but then again, in theory, man can live on the moon.

This is where the cows come in. The rest of Uncle Willie's "parkland ecotone" was crisscrossed by their trails. It was a textbook presentation of edges, sunlit glades, fruit-bearing bushes, and islands of dense brush next to patches of mature trees. The perfect setup for a clean takeoff and a quick turn. Twenty flushes later I was convinced that I had found the grouse's answer to a smooth and easy life.

I figure that I need five flushes to get one opportunity. In Uncle Willie's the flushes were easy; the opportunities were always hard. I kill, on average, about one grouse for every three shots. In Uncle Willie's, one for five was a good day. On that day I got one.

According to game biologists the conditions under which grouse flourish are relatively restricted. It takes the right mix of aspen, spread in a petri dish of controlled clear-cut and divided in age groups that provide brood cover, escape cover, and winter food sources. Uncle Willie's had none of these things. It just had a lot of grouse. A hunter passing by on the township road might glance across the hay field and see a hardwood treeline, but he would only look that way to check the weather. He couldn't see that the wandering ways of a few head of cattle and the annual demands of a wood-burning furnace had created a bird heaven that no biologist could duplicate.

That is what I liked about Uncle Willie's. It proved that good things can happen for no reason. On the south side of Willie's a state-owned parcel was a showcase of management technique. It had all the necessary elements. Clear-cut slash piles, narrow weedy trails lined with eight- to ten-foot-high bristle-brush poplar walls, and enough wasted treetops and cut limbs to stick into your legs going frontwards or backwards. And yet all the grouse were over in Willie's. As soon as they were able they left the slums and went to live in the golf course.

I always loved old maple trees, especially in the fall. I once read that the tree oozes a mild toxin from its roots, causing the small growth around it to retreat. Each one creates a little parkland of its own. When the afternoon sun slants through the blue God's eye of October's sky those yellow-and-red treetops glow like no other in the woods. It must have been trees like this that inspired the architects of cathedral ceilings. At least that is what I was showing my new bride that afternoon. We were hiking the cow trails, talking, walking side by side. In that light everything is beautiful, but she was absolutely radiant.

Cheryl used to hunt with me often in those years before kids. This was one of our favorite places. The fall had been dry and warm, making the cow trails firm and smooth. I had only one dog, my sweet old Lab Dixie. A pointing dog is fired up all the time, like a racing motor that can't idle at low speed. Dixie, on the other hand, took her cue from my mood. We were all very mellow that evening.

There is one main trail to which all the others connect. This path starts at the fence corner, runs along the wire to a great red maple, then turns away from the fence for a short leg, banks sharp right past a hawthorn cluster, through some gray dogwood, and back again to the fence and a gate. We were coming up to the gate when Dixie turned abruptly, dropping her head, to dive to the right. I took one quick step in front of Cheryl, bringing my Model 31 pump up to my cheek at the same time. A grouse flushed away to the left, curling back the way we had come. My first shot was behind, but I regained the lead with a quick slip of the action and dropped the bird within fifteen yards of us.

Dixie had the mark, as usual, and I turned back to ask Cheryl if she had seen the flush. Another bird, on the opposite side of the first, flushed straight away toward the gate, banking to the right and staying just above the brush tops.

Holding the gun out with my left hand, I turned the action so that the ejection window was up. At the same time, I plucked a shell from my cartridge loops with my right hand, flipped the cartridge into the slot, and snapped the slide forward. The grouse was still in range; all I had to do was bring the stock to my cheek and slap the trigger. I didn't miss. It was an Olympic-caliber move.

"Well!" I said, turning around to look into her admiring eyes. "What do you think of that?"

She was bent over with her hands over her ears and her eyes shut. She looked up and blinked, her dark hair falling back into place.

"Did you get anything?" she asked.

I used to like to scout this covert just before the season. The foliage was too dense for any real accurate count, but I always wanted to know what I could expect in the coming fall. This was going to be a record year. I had flushed twenty-five separate birds in the patch between the corner and the gate. Spence Turner was bringing Big Mike for his first hunt on grouse. I was sure that his grand old campaigner would get a noseful.

Mike the setter was eight years old that fall. He was the sire of Spence's line but had never pointed or handled grouse. He was a quail dog, a "big goer." He lacked all the qualities of Samantha, Spence's dam. He was brash, bony, hardheaded, and clownish to boot. He was as subtle as an iron door, and about as big.

Spence loved the old tyrant, and I wanted Spence to be proud. There was no better place to find birds than Uncle Willie's.

Mike found the first covey. There were eight of them all in one lump under the hawthorn bush. I have seen some spectacular rises in my time but never one to equal the feathered explosion that followed Mike's headlong charge into their middle.

Spence was not proud. Mike was not happy. I was awestruck. Eight birds had flown high and open without a good, or even a bad, opportunity. No surprise, because the whole thing happened at about fifty yards. The day did not improve, and Spence was making ugly noises about unwinding Mike's mortal coil.

Two days went by. Sometimes old Mike was in the dog box and other times he was on the ground. It made no difference. The little female, Samantha, and Dixie got all the birds.

"Let's try it one more time, Spence," I said. It was the late afternoon of a cool, sunny day. The wind was steady from the northwest and the rest of the dogs were tired.

"I suppose," he said, pouring a second cup of coffee. "Can't do worse than he has done."

I wasn't so sure. As we walked down the main trail I was giving some thought to where I could stand in order to get some pass-shooting.

Mike was casting wide, but not blind. His bony flank flashed between the trees, and just about the time Spence thought he had gone too far the old setter would appear on the trail and look back.

"He's being a lot more careful, Spence." Lucky thing too, I thought; whenever Spence's eyes got black and squinty, like they were now, he was measuring the range.

Then Mike was gone.

"Mike!" Spence called. "C'mon around!"

There was no Mike. On the other hand there were also no wings whirring.

"Mike! Dammit, c'mon around!" Still nothing.

We walked up the trail, side by side, Spence's head sinking lower into his vest. I had not seen a lot of setters on point, just Samantha, and then only in bits and pieces through the heavy foliage. Mike was in the wide open. He was on POINT! Every fiber of his being from the whiskers on his nose to the tips of his toes said: "Right there!"

It was at the junction of the main trail and two small side tracks. The very same hawthorn patch where he had muffed the job three and a half long days ago.

"Go ahead, Ted." Quiet words—more than a request, less than a command. A pointing-dog man's quiet way of saying "I want to savor this moment forever."

I walked up to within ten yards or so, and stopped. This is a cardinal sin; it can cause the dog to break its concentration, or make the birds move. Nothing happened.

"I wonder if we have an empty hole," I thought. Awful intense for a false point. In a few more steps I was at his side and directly next to the bushes—too close, really.

It was also too close for the grouse. Two birds burst up right under Mike's head, making a double rise so close to my face that I felt the wind from one wing pass my cheek. I fired twice into the air, almost straight up.

"Arrrrgh!" I screamed. "How could I miss that shot!"

Spence was proud. Mike was happy. I was still awestruck.

Cattle prices must have gone up about the time the grouse life cycle went down. Over the next few years the numbers seemed to dwindle. There were fewer birds and more cattle. The cover was getting thinner in the areas where the birds used to hang out. The cattle and I did not get along well. Cows are not bright, but they are territorial and definitely anti-dog. Our last clash in the creek bottom emphasized the need for more space between us.

Two birds had flown the distance downhill from the upland to the dark spruce grove. The cattle were grazing under and around the pines. I had Salty in those last few years, and in typical focused fashion she chased the scent trail to the spruce patch and went on point. A black, middle-sized critter with a huge attitude problem decided to stomp the white dog and came on the run. I charged into the grove from the other side, and we stood and looked at each other.

It huffed and I puffed. Salty pointed, solid and intense. And for a good reason. A grouse was standing on the ground about ten yards in front of her and just to one side of the black bully. The cow came forward, head down and blowing through its nose. I knew enough about cattle to realize this was not a good sign. Salty was resolute. The grouse was indecisive. I was mad.

I walked quickly over to my little setter and took her by the collar in my left hand. Then I leveled the shotgun at the grouse with my right hand. It walked along a bit farther until it was between me and the cow.

A small, and evil, thought formed in my mind. It is wrong to shoot a grouse on the ground. It is also wrong to spray a domestic animal with fine shot. Do two wrongs make a right?

The cow lurched forward. The decision was easy. I grassed the bird and the beast with one blast. Most of the shot charge hit the dirt in front of the cow, but I would like to think that at least a few pellets stung that beefy nose. It spun around and took off with the rest of the herd. I gathered up my dog and bird, and crossed back over the fence. Safe on the other side, I marked the stream cover off of Uncle Willie's inventory.

I found a balloon in the middle of Uncle Willie's. It was still inflated. Inside was a small slip of paper from a Sunday school class in a town almost two hundred miles away. I gave the slip of paper to the teacher of Sunday school in my little church at Maple Hill Lutheran, only about three miles away. The covert had got so thin from cattle grazing that even a thing as fragile as a balloon full of helium could land there and stay intact. I had found other coverts by that time, and I knew by looking around that it was time to say good-bye.

The cows had helped another fellow become friends with Willie and Marlys. This was Joel Vance, an outdoor writer and one of my annual companions from Missouri. A few years before this day he and his son Andy worked the covers with me in the Pedersen surroundings. This makes for a long day, and the sun was setting as we came up to Willie's farm. The cows were out again. Marlys was alone on the road and, while she was doing fine with those few head close by, the bigger and faster types were making an end run. Joel has some of those farm genetics in him, and in a few minutes with my waving and Andy's steady hand he had them turned back into the pasture. We helped restore the fence and visited a bit. In Minnesota you can't just tip your hat and say "proud to help you ma'am."

Joel wouldn't do that anyway. He writes about birds and dogs and the land, but he has his most intense curiosity for people. Intensity is an understatement when one speaks of Vance. Joel is a nerve-ending with arms and legs. He is a living receptor of human impulse. Andy, his son, must have received the restraint that skipped Joel's place in the lineage. Andy is Joe DiMaggio, always under the fly ball no matter where it is hit, standing quietly, punching the pocket in his glove, waiting for it to come down. Joel is Mickey Mantle, running, falling, getting up, hat flying off, and finally leaping into the air to make a spectacular catch.

The result is the same. It's a question of spice.

And, of course, training. Joel has that journalist churning inside. An earthquake is just a bump in the road unless there is a person involved. So he was the guy when it came time to put the wraps on Uncle Willie's.

I chose the last few hours of a nice October afternoon. Instead of parking my old car on one side or another of the farm, I drove up the driveway—level and smooth as always—and stopped in the yard. The old brown dog was gone. No surprise there. It had been fifteen years since my first visit. I knocked on the door. Marlys came into the entry and, recognizing us both, invited us in for coffee.

There are two things common to every farmhouse and church basement in my part of Minnesota. One is hot strong black coffee, and the other is a particular variety of chocolate cake with white frosting. So far as I can determine, every farm or church stove has both of these components from the day it is placed inside until the day it is tossed into the junkpile. And I'll bet that the junkpile stove has an old cake pan inside and an old coffee pot on top.

We drank their coffee and ate the cake. It was, for me, communion at the funeral. Joel knew, or at least sensed, that this visit was our last, and he listened to the stories about the raccoon shot with the cap-and-ball pistol, and the barrel hoop toy. He drank it all in, as did I. We lingered longer than we should have. The sun was setting as we walked across the farmyard to the woodlot gate.

His Brittanies and my setter scoured the open woods with no resistance from brush or bramble. If a grouse had been in there it would have been found. It was not a hunt. It was a wake. A passing of the hands and feet over an old favorite possession, now used up. It was sad, but it was good too. I had to know that the covert had done one good turn.

We were done before dark. I shut the back gate on the dogs and walked to my side of the car. Joel was already sitting inside. I opened the door and sat down. Then I put the key in the ignition and started the motor. The setting sun could now shine through the woods' edge, across the farmyard, and into the car. I turned my head to look back through the rear window as I shifted into reverse and held my gaze on Joel's face long enough to confirm what I knew. It was over. The little car went down the drive, without a bump, and turned left onto the town road.

Chapter 13
Bookends

The township crew probably would have extended the
Pedersen road farther south, but the water of Wood Row Creek
was in front of them, and there was no one living beyond
the farm anyway. So they turned it hard right, and headed
due west. Anyone who wanted to cross the creek knew how
to go through the farm, down to the bridge, and along the
rutted cartway to the next public way. In those days the money
for a road was raised by assessing the adjoining landowners.
The cost of filling and bridging the stream was not likely to
be borne lightly by Scandinavian farmers.

The road ended north at the Olson farm for the same reason.
No farmer—or even a federally funded highway—could afford
to cross the bed of Rice Lake. Bridging the Florida Keys would
have been cheaper. If a bird hunter drove from the Pedersen
farm, up the road, past the Trailer Site, the Disco, and Uncle
Willie's, he had to stop at its intersection with the south side

of the Olson Brothers' farm, because the road didn't go any farther north. About a mile ahead of him, as the crow flies, was a hole named Rice Lake.

We are probably all familiar with those magazine-sized publications called plat books, which set out in picture form the ownership of each segment of land, including the roads and the lakes. Some of them even color the public land green; private land is white, and the lakes are of course blue. The books are useful tools when you want to know where to hunt, and who to ask for permission.

The page covering the land between the beginning of the Pedersen road and the paved public highway at the top shows a great blue oval surrounded by green public land but separated from the township road on each side by white blocks of private land. The big blue oval is Rice Lake. Most of the white belongs to Frank and Walt Olson.

There is no lake in Rice Lake.

There was some clear water there at one time. At least that is what Frank Olson tells me. He ought to know. He and Walt have lived at the farm their whole lives—and, as Frank says, that is so long that he doesn't even buy green bananas anymore. His people came to their farm at the beginning of this century. Frank told me that some government official decided in the 1920s that the best thing to do was to build a ditch and let the water out of the lake. This was done. The ditch is still there today. But this is a bog lake, and a deep one to boot. The water ran out, and is still running. The rest of it stayed. Visions of wheat fields died in official heads. What they left behind was a floating mattress of swamp grass, brush, and shifting potholes.

Sometimes the sight of those big flocks of ducks pitching into the vast open grass of Rice Lake will drive a waterfowler to extreme measures. One fellow tried to walk out to the potholes by strapping on planks. Later another tried it with old wooden water skis. Both men made it back alive, but barely. Teamwork was tried next. An inexhaustible supply of rejected wooden ends for wire spools was available at the dump of a nearby factory. One man carried the reel end (about forty inches wide), the other dropped it down in front of them. In this fashion they made an uneasy walkway of round tiles across the bog to the nearest pothole. Like most plans the theory was sound; it was just the wrong pothole. The ducks were always someplace else.

They could have asked Frank, or Walt, and saved themselves a lot of trouble. The two may seem quaint and creaky now, but in their time there was very little that the two bachelors had not tried. They are the strong bedrock of Scandinavia. While others married away or left to find other work, Frank and Walt stayed on the farm. They lived there with their mother and father until both passed away. There was a plain black 1960 Ford in the machine shed for all the years I knew them. It was used to take their mom to church. In those days it was unseemly to arrive at the First Norwegian Lutheran Church in a pickup truck. It is okay now. Maybe the name change to Maple Hill Lutheran Church did it, or perhaps the fact that most pickups these days cost as much, if not more, than a car.

At any rate, wars came and went. The local boys did their part. Frank went into World War II. So also went Walt Pedersen, into the infantry, and from there to Honeywell and the space program. Frank came back. Then it was Walt Olson's turn to go to Korea. Walt came back too, but not entirely. He left a piece of his skull and his left eye on one of those muddy ridges. He was also left—for dead. But these men are strong stock. Walt survived. In fact, he did better than that. A couple years ago he returned to the V.A. hospital complaining of dizziness and headaches. Expecting the worse, they opened up his old wound and found the steel plate crumpled by the new bone that grew over the hole. The surgeon removed the plate and sewed him up. It takes a damn good Norwegian to grow a new head.

Birds and bird dogs don't mean much to the Olson Brothers. They love the land, and trapping. Walt is sure death to the pocket gopher. He is retired now, and yet every day that weather permits he is out on his all-terrain vehicle, patrolling the pastures. And watching. Nothing passes through this land without his gaze. Frank likes to catch the beaver in the government ditch drain. They aren't worth anything these days, but, as he would tell you over coffee in the kitchen, it gives him something to do now that the cows are gone.

The Olsons retired twice. The first time was an act of God. The herd was grazing in the open pasture next to the jack-pine grove. About milking time, a sudden summer storm came in and lightning struck the grove. Walt went out (on his all-terrain, as usual) to get the cows. He drove through the herd—all on their backs, legs up in the air—without stopping. Into the barn he went, and pulled up to where Frank was putting feed into the stalls.

"Vell, ders no need to do dat, Frank, dey are all dead."

I never did find out what Frank said in return, but chances are he dusted off his hands, put the pitchfork away, and returned to the house for a cup of coffee.

One thing led to another, however, and the insurance check became two or three cows at the auction barn. Then another three or four because, "Dey are yust too good to pass up."

And they *were* too good to pass up. Frank proved it when a fellow came into their barn during milking time, looked around, and offered him a top sale price on the spot.

"Yu yust bot yerself a herd, mister." And time got on Frank's hands.

He cuts wood for the furnace and splits it to pile in the pasture. Row upon row of clean white chunks, waiting for a trip to the basement.

For fun, he still goes down to the government ditch. Sometimes he traps the beaver. Sometimes he places a little dynamite in the dam and blows it sky high.

I'd like to see you do that in the city.

I think that my young English setter, Dots, was the first bird dog that either Frank or Walt ever got involved with. She was a living fire. When I trained her in the field next to my house, cars would stop and the people in them would watch her sweep across the tall grass like a whirlwind. She was the living symbol of speed and beauty. A tall white tail flowing behind a chiseled angular head. Below her straight back the muscles rippled, driving her legs like a fine racehorse. She was intoxicating to watch, and I worked with her almost every evening in preparation for the opening of grouse season. It was to be her first full year hunting and she was destined to be Salty's heir apparent.

Control was a problem, but nothing insurmountable. She was a little crazy, hurling herself through the brush, and sometimes she was slow to return when I blew the whistle. Like the first time my son, Max, and I took her out to the Olson Brothers. I had left work early with the intention of taking both pups, human and canine, for a bit of exercise and some woods time, but I noticed that she was gone shortly after we started a walk along the pasture edge. It was just Max and me at the tail end of an October afternoon.

One of the great advantages of the Olson Brothers covert is that it has a wide variety of habitat. The east side is upland and lowland mixed, with a blend of pasture openings and small tongues of brush leading out from these places. It is a perfect place to walk without a heavy effort, and at the same time it affords a pretty good opportunity to shoot a grouse loafing along the clover edges.

Dots must have scented one of these birds and followed her nose into the alders. When I found her, she was looking up into the branches. I followed her gaze and saw two grouse perched out of reach and staring back at her with equal interest. I had left Max on the trail, out of harm's way, so I was free to shoot in any direction. I walked forward, past Dots, and both birds took off, climbing up into the yellow treetops.

I caught the trailing grouse with the shot charge and saw it tumble into a heavy patch of leafy screen. I did not get a very good line on the exact place.

Max and I searched, and Dots was there from time to time, although without much enthusiasm. The bird was lost. I sat down and took my pipe from my pocket, packing the old tobacco down with new, and mumbled about my miserable luck. Max was still poking around, and Dots was nowhere close.

The effort was fruitless, and the moment spoiled. I stood up and walked over toward Max, hoping to run into Dots on the way. I could see him, but she was gone. I put my whistle in my mouth and turned around to blow a "c'mon back." She was standing behind me, with her first grouse in her mouth. I had a genius just coming to bloom!

The first cool evening of the following August I had in mind a repeat performance. No birds would be shot, but there was an excellent chance for another productive point. I had bought her a bell of her own the year before. It was one of those brass types with a spring latch at the top allowing it to be hung on the collar ring. She lost it within the first ten minutes.

It was called The Perfect Dog Bell in the advertisement. I ordered another bell, the more conventional hang-from-the-collar type, and while placing the order with the same supplier, I complained to the clerk.

"She lost it within the first hundred yards of cover," I said.

"That's why it's called The Perfect Dog Bell," he responded.

I put Salty's bell on Dots that late summer's eve. It was a bronze ringer with a sound that carried for a quarter mile on a quiet day.

She was belled and primed to go. Max stepped out of the way and Dots cleared the first fifteen feet off the tailgate of the truck before hitting the ground. She swung wide to the left, through a small woodlot, then swept back across the trail heading to the right. Her bell was bright and clear, then fainter and fainter. She was out of sight and sound before I realized her direction was directly toward the soggy jungle of Rice Lake.

I blew the whistle long and hard, and waited. I listened for the bell. It was quiet, windless, she could not run without making that clear musical tone. My hearing has reached that stage where I have a permanent chorus of crickets as background music. I asked Max if he could hear the bell. There was no sound carrying back from the bog.

We got in the truck and drove around the pasture edge, climbing to the top of the highest hill. We got out and I blew the whistle again and again. Max listened and I blew the tune. About a year before, when Dots was a stringy pup, she took a run through the edge of the old lake bed. I could just barely keep track of her, but I remember how surprised I was to see the speed with which she could cover that dense and difficult ground. A deer could not have run it better.

It was almost full dark when I left a blanket and some food on the ground where we first dropped her off. I had never left a dog in the woods. I could see her caught in a coyote snare. I was imagining her fear and loneliness and the panic that must be gripping her as tightly as fear held me. Max and I drove out of the field gate and down the road to the farmhouse.

It was a lovely evening for sitting out under the stars. The kind we all remember as kids sitting on the porch under the yellow glow of bug lights. The yellow light bulbs of A&W Root Beer stands and county fair midways. Frank and Walt were sitting on their wooden park bench. The one by the weather vane. Frank on one end, Walt on the other. Sitting in the dark, like bookends. Between them was fat old Holly, their standard-issue brown farm dog.

Max and Holly went off into the yard to do boy and dog things. I took her place. We said nothing for a while. A nighthawk buzzed the pickup looking for a snack.

"I lost my dog," I said.

"Dah hell yu did! Vas it dah little white vun?" Walt asked.

"No, it was the new one, the pup. I was working her in the east pasture next to the lake bed."

"Oh das too bad," Frank answered. "She'll come back, yu bet."

"I don't think so. She's a damn fool. Her answer to everything is to run faster. I think she's done it this time, boys. The old dog always used her head first and never forgot where she came from. This one can't seem to hold a thought long enough to act on it."

"Vhere vas she going, Ted?" Walt asked.

"I'm not sure, but the only direction she could go and still stay hidden was right out into the bottom of that lake bed. I put Salty's bell on her. Right now that's what I'd like to have back."

Frank's voice had a smile in it. "Let's valk over behind dis machine shed and lissen out across dat field. Dos neighbor cows are out der and if she pops out dey vill start to hollar."

Every homestead I have ever found has two common plants: plum trees and lilacs. It's almost as if the land agent handed out the seedlings with every deed. Their grove was behind the shed and next to the big field. We stood in the darkening gloom listening and watching until the white shapes of the dairy cows became lumps on gray hills.

"Vell, furst ting in dah morning I vill take dah tree-wheeler and check dos far fields," said Walt. I knew that if a white dog could be found in this piece of ground it was as good as done. First thing in the morning to Walt and Frank Olson means an hour before sunup.

She wasn't found. Two and a half days later I got a call from a farm wife. My dog had turned up in their ditch, alive. Dots had been attracted by the noise of her children waiting for the school bus.

"I could tell by the collar and the bell that she was probably lost," she said. "I fed her and she's here in the house with me 'bout half starved."

I drove out to get her immediately. The lady of the house refused any money, and accepted my thanks in the fashion of country people, depreciating her efforts as "nothing special."

I stopped at Frank and Walt's on the way home.

"So, dat's dah vun," said Frank, his face grinning widely. "I tell yu she gave us a run!"

"Boy, I guess so!" agreed Walt. "We wus up every morning calling and looking. Hell, I run all dos trails tru dos voods. An dah neighbor and I looked eff'ry place a dog could hide." I got a hearty slap on the back and all thanks turned aside.

I am not mocking the way my friends speak. Their language is the flavor of this land. A few years before this day, my good Missouri friends were taking their lunch in the sunny pasture. We had been shooting regularly enough to attract Walt's undivided attention. He motored up on his three-wheeler and turned off the engine. We spoke for an hour or so on the local events, enjoying some common gossip. When he left, my favorite Southern boy of the bunch rolled up on his elbow from where he had been pretending to take a nap.

"Ah jist luv to lizzen to him talk," he drawled. "Heez got sech a nice acksent."

The Olson Brothers covert is perfectly named. It would be nothing without them. They have cut the trees, created the edges, and farmed in the rough style it takes to pull a hard-earned living from this rocky land. Between the two of them, they have made a place for the birds, and the men who hunt them. They didn't intend to do anything other than raise a few dairy cows and some hay. But good things happen between men who are solid as bookends.

Chapter 14
More

The key to Frank and Walt's gate was a museum piece. It reminded me of those Old West jail-lock keys that are always being lifted from the pockets of sleeping deputies. It had a long iron shank with a cloverleaf of open circles at one end. Attached to this was a leather tag from an old watch fob. On the other end a thick blade had been forged with one big notch. The shank was hollow in order to fit around a pin in the lock. The padlock was proportional to the key. If there is a lock on the gates of hell, or heaven, it must look like this one: big, rusty, heart-shaped iron with a small door covering the key port. When the key was slipped in and over the spindle, it would turn with a wonderful creak and the hasp would pop open. The locks on all the really fine things in life should look, sound, and work this way.

I didn't always come in through this gate. When I first started to hunt these sixteen hundred acres I crossed through the land of another owner. He had a small grass pasture farther west from where the Pedersen road meets the bottom of the Olson Brothers. It was a new place to me then, and I had yet to meet Frank and Walt.

The owner was a tall, severe-looking man, one of the several proud sons of a lay minister of the gospel. Their father was no Lutheran. He had his own ideas about salvation and he was proud to share them with anyone he spoke to. A short stop to ask permission to hunt his land might be answered yes, or no, depending on your cut, but every inquirer left with a small religious tract in his hand, taken from the man's pocket and passed over to save your soul. A massive mission in this country.

Looks can be deceiving. My acquaintance (the lay-minister's son), though tall, dark, and somber, had a merry twinkle in his eye. He was a poet, philosopher, and the living repository of a world of local lore. He and his brothers, like the Pedersens and the Olsons, lived well in the sand and pine of their county, taming the land and its denizens equally.

When I asked to hunt his land he related a story about a bird of a different feather. "My brother Gaylord had a pet crow," he began. "It was curious about everything. One day he got to do the laundry because of it. The sheets were boiled in those days in a big scalder over an open fire outside. Once they were white enough, my mother would pick them out with a stick and feed the end into a double roller that was turned with a crank. The sheet would run through the rollers, wringing out the water, and then curl end over end into a tub. Gaylord was doing the turning and his crow was walking around in the mud next to the boiler. The bird got to looking at that long clean white conveyor belt of cotton coming out of the wringer. He hopped up on it and left his muddy tracks along the laundry while keeping up with the progress of the cloth as it fell into the tub. Mother saw it first. The broom sent the crow in one direction, and Gaylord in the other."

He laughed until the tears welled up in his eyes. "Gaylord got to do the laundry all over again, whether it was clean or dirty.

"Anyway, you go ahead, and cross through that pasture if you want. I may look in on you from time to time."

I found a path, part deer trail and part tote road. It took me in the direction I wanted to go, more or less, and every path invites exploration anyway. It turned out to be a pretty productive edge on its own. The first one hundred yards or so were heavy with the sunshine-loving bushes and berries found in any field edge, but the whole thing seemed to hold only two grouse.

It was common to flush the two grouse one at a time, but I seldom got a clear shot. They would fly on ahead into the jack-pine grove. I was always ready for them. On the other hand, they always seemed ready for me. Thus I had settled on a habit of early failure. The scenario was the same, time after time: Flush the birds, follow the flush, stand for a moment scratching my head, move on to where my path intersected the main trail. Then one of the two made a fatal error. He perched in the pine tree under which I was standing. I paused long enough to unhinge his nerve, and he broke out of the tree limbs giving me a snap shot.

I watched, and listened, but there had been no indication of a hit and no sound of a fall. About two hours later, Dixie and I returned from our long walk north. Dixie never loafed; her bird-finding button was always on. My mind was on the field out ahead. As I walked along, I could hear her breathing in a peculiar way behind me. I stopped and turned. She was standing, patiently, with the grouse in her mouth. I examined it and found that it had been hit in the head and apparently had towered up into the pine branches and gotten hung up for a while. The dog had searched very thoroughly the first time. I considered myself lucky to have made the shot. The rest was just the experience and persistence of a fine dog.

I visited the pasture entrance often in those first years of exploration. My faithful transportation was well known to all, a rusted out, bent-fendered Toyota station wagon held together with duct tape and bumper stickers. One fall morning I had a hunting companion and we drove out in his car, parked it in the same spot, and went down the path into the woods. A few hours later we returned. There was a note under the driver's wiper. It said:

"Ted, if this is you, pay no attention, if it isn't, get out!"

My little pasture entrance became a homesite for the owner's daughter. I was still welcome to park there, but the presence of a basement home and the inevitable barking dog or two made my old practice more like an intrusion. I was self-conscious about shooting at birds around the house, and I like to take my lunch in peace. The constant yap of her excited ankle-biters reminded me of the office telephone, and I came out here to be rid of that. It was time to find a new home. It was this change that brought me to the door of Frank and Walt Olson. I never had a chance to thank her for moving in, and as to the two grouse on the field path, well, the loss of the chance to chase them was a fair trade for what I was about to discover.

Being able to go through the Olsons' gate changed everything. A little two-rut trail was scratched into the grass of the field. It wound past the brothers' cornfield, then through a second gate, down a long hill around a point of woods, and then sharp left to cross a shallow ditch. I often stopped right here. It was warm and sunny and the ditch was a drain from a small creek that ran through a wooded lowland.

There was one particular woodcock that lived right at the very tip of the alders that lined the creek. He was there as regularly as a traffic cop on a street corner. Salty was so used to his location that she would jump from the car, hustle over to the bushes, and point. He was where he was supposed to be, and it became a habit. We never shot him. I considered him to be the mascot for a section of the Olson Brothers covert that I called, in recognition of its most prominent citizen, Leonard Woodcock.

I had a lot of fun with that name because it exemplified the nature of the place itself. One of my companions once asked me how it came to be called by a man's name instead of a feature or location. I replied, "Leonard Woodcock was the head of the UAW, one of the most powerful unions in the world. He said that the wants of his constituency could be summed up in one four-letter word: More!"

That, I explained, was exactly what the covert was all about. It had more brush, more fallen logs, more tangle foot, and more woodcock than any other place I had ever been in...while grouse hunting.

There are rumors of bird hunters who only seek woodcock. I gave those reports the same credibility as another writer once put rumors of Bigfoot, lower taxes, and affordable health care. I pass up woodcock, pausing only to keep my pact with Salty to shoot at, or near, every fifth one. It keeps her from sulking over unrewarded points. If there is a bird hunter who can pass up an opportunity at a flushing grouse I haven't been with him. I won't be. The doodle is amusing to dogs, young hunters, and people who fancy liver. I understand and appreciate all these things. But anyone who would disdain a shot at the king of upland birds needs therapy that I cannot comprehend.

I am as connected to the grouse as a goshawk. It is my singular passion. I used to wonder why I stopped in one place, or turned left or right in another. I stopped wondering and consigned the thought to instinct. A perfect example of my connection to the grouse happened right in the Leonard Woodcock covert.

The covert is made up of two bowls, like a figure eight, with perhaps twenty acres in each. The sides are high ridges with groves of tall lodgepole white pines on a couple sides, some spruce along the others. The centers of the bowls were clear-cut for the poplar, and in the bottom of the far bowl a wet swamp of black, stunted spruce forms a boundary along an alder slough. In another corner the ash trees have shaded out most of the undergrowth, providing a lush green park and a nice place to rest.

It has been ten or so years since the cutting, and the poplar saplings have grown in lush profusion wherever their parent trees were taken. Foresters count this sort of regrowth by stems per foot, but I can tell you that a shotgun cannot be swung in this hairbrush density. It comes down to picking a spot and shooting into it.

The woodcock are cooperative, if a hunter is of a mind to take one. They rise up to a peak and pause for a moment of indecision. Having made up its mind the bird drops a load of whitewash and either dies, because the shooter found a slot to follow him, or fades only to land twenty yards away. A grouse knows how to use interference. He runs out of the heavy traffic, sets his course, and bores low and hard, twisting around the big trees, flying to avoid becoming a meal. A person doesn't read much about the woodcock as a prey for anything. They fly like that. Sort of like butterflies that taste bad. No grouse dies of old age. They all end up on some creature's plate, and they act like it.

It was a Friday afternoon. I had left the office early and traded my shirt, tie, and respectability for the kind of clothes that hard-working men wear to the barn. I was about midway on the first side, looking down through the yellow poplar screen for a glimpse of Salty or Dixie. I could hear the setter's bell coming back on a return route and I was certain that old Dixie was shagging after the woodcock that I had just bumped into the air. It occurred to me that I should turn left. The decision was not a logical process of weighing all the alternatives. It just seemed like the natural thing to do. A couple of poplar stumps had formed a clump of saplings and invited a brief stop. If the scene had been videotaped the operator would have slipped into slow motion at this point. There was a grouse nearby; I knew it as surely as a fox stalks a mouse.

The situation was impossible. A heavy wall of foliage was directly in front of me, on both sides, and I had just walked through the only opening. I raised my gun and, at the same time, stepped backward very slowly. That was enough to spook him. He came up off the ground only ten or twelve feet from my left foot. I saw him as a red crescent with a sharp black band along the edge. Each white spot was bright against the dark brown back. There were no wings, just two gray blurs and some bits of flying leaf debris. He was gone. Suddenly, he was back in a small opening, not as a whole bird but rather as an object in motion. A burst of energy moving things out of the way.

I didn't calculate angles. If I was aware of mounting the gun, it wasn't by any conscious thought. The bird was part of one seamless motion, both of us flowing in the same direction. He was completely out of sight when I shot. The place that my eyes saw was a cloud of pellets vaporizing a patch in the cover between us. But I knew he was in that mist of lead and leaves. I have had that experience before. All of us have. We know when it happens because the first sensation is a return of sound. It is as if, for a thousandth of a second, all sound went rushing out toward that pinpoint of concentration.

The next sensation is a deep breath. After that, things fall into their usual routine. The gun has to be opened, the empty shell extracted, and another load put in its place.

My shot brought both dogs back to check on me.

"Over there, girl," I gestured with my right hand, "it flew that way."

We walked together. The dogs are experienced enough to follow along until I stop and tell them to "hunt dead." This was not one of their birds, it was mine, and they had to wait for directions. None were necessary. It lay against a fallen log, its head and chest pressed to the side, wings extended, and the great red tail still fully spread in a black-tipped crescent pressing against the yellow grass.

I wish I could say that I sat down on the log and took deep appreciation in all of the unique qualities of that moment. Some more creative writers could draw analogies to the classics in art and philosophy. Those with a bent toward Eastern mythology could probably describe in painstaking detail the precise Zen position that was assumed and the meditation which followed. I didn't feel any of those things which would have inspired a more insightful author. I picked up the bird and put it in my game pouch. I wasn't even poetic enough to smooth the feathers and feel the warm weight and so on. The only thing I can say in my defense is that I did not say "neat."

I thought it; I just didn't say it.

And I wanted to do it again. Which only goes to prove, I guess, that some of the most significant experiences in life pass right by us at the time they happen.

I am an occasional pipe smoker. I like the aroma of the tobacco, and the nice way that pipe-smoking details fill up awkward moments while I am thinking of something to say. There used to be a pipe called a "yellow bowl," named after its colored lining. That is what I called this part of the Leonard Woodcock. Poplar saplings grow fast and straight. The first year they hold on to their big green leaves well into late October. The grouse favor green food above the buds and catkins. If a hunter slips into one of the new clear-cuts in the late afternoon he can, on occasion, find a covey feeding out in the open. It makes for fast shooting. Most of the time, however, the little trees press on toward the sun in a head-long race to reach above each other. Within about eight or ten years the clear-cut will have formed a hairbrush-thick mass of tall sticks, about as big as your thumb, with a thick leafy top. A really fine wood-producing cut will show stems so close together that a man could not fall down without twisting around a bit.

The Yellow Bowl was about mediocre in the wood-products division. The regrowth was patchy, leaving room to walk around under the canopy, which was absolutely first-rate in the creation of the color "glowing yellow." It is a common cliché in outdoor writing to expound on the "golden coins of aspen leaves spilling down" in describing those magical few days in October when all the poplar turn color and a rain has not stripped the trees. The Yellow Bowl was open to the west and was the place to be when a late-afternoon sun laid its rays across the poplar tops.

Somewhere in every camera bag there is a yellow No. 2 filter. Photographers like to use this as a mood setter. It gives a photograph a timeless, warm quality. The color of life filtered through the glowing screen of poplar tops is even softer, quieter. When I stand in the corners of this place I am reminded of underwater movies shimmering the color of the sea on coral reefs.

Just before sundown the warm, used-up air of the day is pushed up from the bottoms of the Yellow Bowl. I was walk-ing downhill, deliberately, seeking out the small pockets of cool evening to feel the difference. Salty was under the false impression that we were grouse hunting. She was hunting, I was goofing off. It was a Wednesday and my court hearing had concluded early. I had made that clothing trade again and was seeking the pleasant tightness in my stomach that comes from too much fun. She moved through the clusters of poplar and tall grass, sampling the rising air. Above us there was no sky, just an overhead ceiling of glowing yellow. The large fallen trees were dark, and the shadows more intense than in the early afternoon.

I had my 12-gauge Parker shotgun with me, the same gun that I used to shoot the impossible grouse of the previous week. It was, and still remains, my main gun. It is heavy in comparison to my Westley Richards 20-gauge, and weighted toward the barrel, unlike my favorite Model 31 pump. I had it restocked with a glorious piece of New Zealand walnut, but in the same dimensions as the old stock—in other words, crooked as a hockey stick. But it is like an old ball player or an experienced hunting dog, ungainly to look at, until the game starts. Then all those odd angles come together into an efficient and deadly tool.

Salty made a sudden and dramatic point. One moment she was moving and the next she was frozen in midstride. Her gaze was fixed on a grouse. It was standing at the end of a long, dark, fallen log. The bird did not move, certain that it was safe.

I make a regular habit out of missing this shot. I think about it too much. I remember all the other grouse that flew away after a two-shot salute. I moved to my left, hoping to get a better angle and perhaps cause it to flush out and away instead of straight across. I flushed a second bird on the other side of the big log and it fell, shot stone dead. Instinctively, I pivoted back to take the open grouse with the second barrel. It was still frozen in place. It had taken a short step away from the log, but Salty had stopped it with a corresponding move of her own.

Those two-shot salutes preyed on my mind. I opened the gun, and I got away with plucking the empty out of the open barrel and slipping another shell in! I took two more steps, leading with my left foot, planning the whole thing carefully. A third grouse flushed just behind me.

All I had to do was turn from the waist, swing the Parker from right to left, catch up, and press the front trigger. The old gun throws a pattern that is elliptical, or lozenge-shaped, right to left. The bead was just behind the double crescent wings but the grouse fell, straight down, turning a somersault in the air.

Two birds down, and I had yet to walk three feet! I swung back to take the pointed grouse. It had heard enough. It was a beanball in the air, midway between its takeoff spot and my head. I missed on the incoming chance and had no cartridge for the going away.

The two down birds were easy finds. Old Dixie was resting that afternoon, having hurt her neck retrieving a duck. Salty would not retrieve, but if I begged and stayed cool she would seek out the dead ones and stand over the spot. I picked up both of them, put the opened gun across the big log, laid the birds next to the Parker, and sat down. Salty stood patiently, wagging her tail, ready to go.

I took my pipe out of my vest and packed it slowly with tobacco, then lit the bowl with a kitchen match, holding it with my fingers and striking the tip with my thumbnail. It worked on the first try.

Pipe smoking has a lot to recommend it. Especially when the clouds of fragrant smoke drift light and yellow in the cool evening air.

Leonard Woodcock was right: more is better.

Chapter 15

Birds in Seisin

Under our law, the word *seisin* has no defined meaning. In the common law of England it meant possession of a piece of land as a holding free from the claim of the feudal lord. Hence the name *freeholder*. Transfer of ownership was accomplished by the passing of a piece of sod or clump of earth from the parcel to be seised to the freeholder who intended to take possession. It seems a quaint custom now, but in those times all land belonged to the king, and very few people knew how to read and write. The common man was most often nothing more than a tenant or vassal, and until the Magna Carta was imposed upon the king, land ownership was entirely at the whim of the reigning lord. This old doctrine of "corporeal investiture" is no longer in force. Now that most people can read and write, delivery of a deed gives seisin in the law.

If all this seems like a long stretch to justify a title pun, trust me. The doctrine of divine ownership through territorial seisin has deep cultural roots and is still with us, though no longer defined by possession so much as by exclusion. It is fortunate for today's freeholder that the vast majority of the population can read. Otherwise those No Trespassing and Keep Out signs would have as little practical value as a deed in the hands of an illiterate peasant.

My point is that the money some folks make in the city has found its way back to the woods. They have bought their little parcel, posted it against intrusion, and have apparently the same feelings for their "forty up north" as they have for their kids, spouse, or dog. Criticism is rarely welcome.

I will risk it, however, for there is hardly a chance that the owners of the forty-acre square on the edge of the Olson Brothers will ever read these words. I suspect there is more than one owner, though I have never seen them. I have found five deer stands constructed in that neighborhood. The semi-trailer standing in the clearing appears to be a dwelling of sorts. I would like to talk to them, but I doubt that we share much except for the land. Our link on that ground is only physical. They wait upon the deer. I seek the grouse. They scatter plastic jugs, junk, and debris. I pick it up and pile it under the trailer.

I wonder if the Freeholder knows about the covey that lives in the second bowl of the Leonard Woodcock so close to his border. I doubt it, because city folks don't wander far from the road. The second bowl lies between the town-ship gravel and the other cover I call the Yellow Bowl. If a person was oriented to the road I suppose he would argue that the second should be the first, given its closer proximity to the gravel. But I count the road as the last place I want to be. If it were not for the covey, I would spend no time there at all.

I guess that makes me a poacher in the Freeholder's eyes. Some of the second bowl is his seisin. But since I don't seek the king's deer I qualify only in the sense that I move quietly, after assuring myself that he is not at the castle and I will cause him no concern.

Freeholder knows by his trash pile that I visit the camp. But he keeps his signs on the road to warn away others who would enter from there. If he were concerned about me he would paper the woods as well. I leave a tailfeather plucked from the home covey in his trailer lock so that he knows my business.

The outside edge of the second bowl is formed by a grass slough and the road ditch, but more prominently by a second ridge at the roadside. This high land runs along the right-of-way and then fades off into the open pasture of Freeholder's semitrailer. Somewhere in between lies the boundary for the line of his holding and the state's ground.

The timber cutters weren't concerned when they laid the trees down. My guess is that the forty was owned by one of them, because its opening is actually an old log landing and skid site. The logs went away and the semitrailer came in.

Pursuant to state instructions a fringe of big pines and hardwoods was left along the road. The new lumberjacks operate on rubber tires, and when they are done the slash is piled neatly in one corner and the stumps are clipped off at ground level. The work done on this parcel was in the old-fashioned style, in the days before hydraulic shears and heavy equipment, which means that there is a ring of felled but uncut trees mixed in with the border brush and slash. It would make a pretty fair palisade for a fort.

The home covey knows this. These grouse may grow up in the middle among the dense, straight poplar saplings, but when they are old enough to fly they move out to the edge. Bird biologists speculate that the brood mother isn't all that caught up in child care once the chicks are hatched. Maybe so, but those words are written in square, clean rooms. I can tell you that the grouse in this covey know the best protection lies where a hunter can't get both feet on the ground.

When the dogs and I have combed and scuffled through the Yellow Bowl, we sit down here on the shared ridge and have a smoke. We rest and recollect the memories of where we're going next. If I have a hunting partner or two, and if they are old comrades with some experience in this place, the same thing happens for a few minutes before we start. We put new shells in empty loops, button pocket flaps, retie boot laces, check straps, open guns, and dust off barrels. Such is the universal ritual of old soldiers who know the nature of the place and the adversary they will meet there.

We stay within sight of one another, moving slowly; one stops, the other walks. This is not trolling for a bite. The grouse are here. The dogs know it; they move the same way— walk a few yards, point, readjust, seek the scent again—trying to cut off the running bird. Finally, one of the dogs locks down solid. If we are lucky we can see the point and whistle a soft *bob-white* to the near man. I haven't seen a pointed bird in here but I have the image of one in my mind. It is crouched with its body low and close to the ground. Its head turns from side to side and those bright brown eyes are trying to find the hunter coming up beside the dog. The escape is all planned. The grouse just doesn't know if the hunter will walk by this time.

If the hunter hasn't seen the dog he will walk by. If he has seen the dog he will pause, and that will be enough to unhinge the bird. Either way, the flush will be low, under the leaf cover, then up on top to see the far edge, and back down into the screen. Most important (at least to the grouse), it must start from the outside of the palisade, then up over the tangle, and back down into the middle ground.

I have seen one bird do it; I have seen five do it. I don't care what the biologists say—mother didn't raise any dummies. The best a man and a dog can hope for in here is a mistake and maybe a good piece of teamwork that gets one of the hunters out in front.

There is a big pile of limbs interwoven with creeper vines that has resisted the poplar growth. If a man can get to this place before his partner moves the covey he may have an opportunity to take a good shot. Old Salty once worked a running bird back and forth in the slash, setting and resetting her points until the grouse stopped to rethink its escape. The bird was in the open edge of the pile. Salty held it long enough for me to climb over the logs and get my feet under me. The little setter was to my left, just in sight, her gaze fixed and intense. Dixie was watching her partner just as intensely. I didn't have to wade in after the bird.

"Get 'im!" I snapped. The black streak going in was followed by a gray-brown form coming up and out, reaching for the sky. A bad mistake. It was one of those shots that you take to your heart and carry with you forever. I saw every feather, and a bright glistening eye. The barrels moved out in front. At the shot, the bird's wings snapped tight around its body, but it flew on like a football spiral, slipping through the poplar stems and landing cleanly a few yards away.

There is only one other wounded bird that I remember as clearly. I was hunting with one of my Missouri partners and we had chased and reflushed a single bird three times, pushing it to the far edge of the Freeholder's clearing. My companion walked out to the opening and probed along its side. I stayed in the woods, which were composed of middle-age poplar with a grassy undergrowth. There was no place left to hide. Puzzled by the bird's disappearance I turned back, intending to retrace my steps to the last flush. I heard wings in front of me and watched the grouse come up off the grass. It flew in a rising but straight line past my shoulder and directly toward the opening.

"Bird's up!" I hollered, then followed its flight with my shotgun and pressed the trigger. The bird was hit, but not fatally. It faded off its climb and slid in a downhill stall until it slammed into the side of the semitrailer with a grand "whank!"

I walked over to the trailer and picked up the limp fugitive, now stone dead. "A kamikaze grouse," I said to my friend. "We ought to put these trailers up all over the woods."

Freeholder and his friends are afraid of getting lost. They have cut trails to each deer stand and have tied orange tape along the trees to find their way back. I help them refresh their memory by cutting the tape each year and rolling it up neatly under their trailer. All their stands and trails are on state land anyway, and my interpretation of a "wilderness experience" is certainly as valid as theirs. The trails, however, do serve a purpose: they organize the trackless space adjacent to the two bowls so that I can give clear instructions to those who hunt with me.

The main path leads downhill from the opening and goes past a little hill upon which four spruce trees grow in one clump. This place is called Turner's Knees. Two things happen here every fall on the first day of the Missouri-clan hunt.

It will be in the early afternoon. Spence Turner, my other Missouri visitors, and I will have finished the long pull through Leonard Woodcock, the Yellow Bowl, and the second bowl. We will be walking single file down the trail, and when we reach the four pines a grouse will flush on its own or off a point. I plan to stop here one of these seasons and say "pull" to commemorate its predictability. The bird always escapes and coasts downhill, cutting to the right around the first grove of ash trees and fleeing back into the lower part of the Yellow Bowl.

This will be Turner's first afternoon of hard walking after—in his words—"a quiet summer." His round body will grind to a halt in its usual tanklike fashion and he will say, "Boys, my knees are giving out. Which way back to the cars?"

He is serious. His knees are only one of a number of physical ailments. I am sympathetic to his desire to cut the walk short, and after a conference on where he is in relation to where he wants to be, we split up. He gathers his two setters, one under each arm, and sits down to "rest a bit for the trip back." I offer to go with him and he waves me off with a wish for my good luck.

In about twenty minutes I will expect to hear his little 20-gauge cracking off in sharp two-shot bursts. He has a perversion. He loves to hunt the woodcock in the Yellow Bowl. Once I am on my way, he can putter around with his fine pointing dogs until the sun sets the yellow poplar tops ablaze.

The rest of the trail continues down the ridge into the ash swamp, which has shaded away the dense undergrowth. A decision has to be made. I can keep going straight, skirt the water-filled holes along the black spruce thicket, and take the dry ground rising on the other side. This direction will put me into a fine grouse cover between the swamp and a clear-cut. But I will miss hunting the Snow Plow unless I turn sharply left and push through a very heavy fringe of alder and doghair poplar—always a difficult and exhausting effort. The Snow Plow covert, however, is worth it. The bit of reserve energy I feel in my legs convinces me to turn left; I can hunt that other cover on the way back.

Going through this piece of ground is like probing for a splinter with a sharp needle. It feels good to be done with it. I am working toward an open area that is now a pine tree plantation. Years ago, when I hunted this parcel from the little pasture entry, the alder swamp was bordered by mature poplar. That was the year before my American water spaniel was killed by a poacher's trap. I had borrowed a gun from a new friend who had lent it to me after I had expressed an interest in lightweight double-barrel 20-gauges. The spaniel and I came to the edge of the alders and I paused for a moment to gather the energy for the plunge. The little spaniel pressed on ahead. I was standing in the clear, able to look down into the cover. A grouse flushed and came out to my right, climbing straight and fast to escape the little brown dog. I brought the 20 to my shoulder and missed, twice. In just about the time it took to reload, a second grouse made the same flight. I missed twice more. It got worse. I stood in that spot and missed seven consecutive grouse, each flushed one at a time. I consider it fortunate that the dog was not much of a retriever.

Then the poplar trees were cut. I came into the cover from the Olson Brothers' side in mid-December, climbing out of the alder swamp to stare in dumbfounded wonder at the wide expanse where woods used to be. Their absence was made even more poignant by the snow on the ground. An entire cover was gone except for the swamp. As I walked around the edge of the clear-cut I came upon the plow that the tree cutters had used to push the snow. It was a homemade V plow, crude, rusty, and now abandoned—pushed to the side and left for scrap. From that day forward it was my landmark for this place.

At first I had no reason to return. The poplar was not allowed to regrow. The land was scraped clean and pine trees were planted. But of course grouse love edges. In a couple years, the woods bordering the cut were fringed in sun-loving berries like the gray dogwood. The trail made for the log trucks intersected a second trail and in this fashion made more edge and more grouse food. One of the biggest clumps of gray dogwood berries in the whole sixteen hundred acres grew up around the old snow plow. It became a magnet for more than rust; it drew grouse in coveys.

I suppose when there are that many birds in a spot one of the bunch will be retarded. I am glad this doesn't happen often, because a grouse as impaired as the one that roosted in the tree above the old snow plow could ruin the reputation of the entire covey.

My two companions and I were reorganizing after a short turn through a dogwood cluster when the bird fluttered up from in front of the rusty hulk, lighting on a lone limb sticking out of the tall bare trunk of a white pine. The grouse sat on the stub and gazed down at the assembled dogs and men, as unconcerned as a barn pigeon. This bird was the living example of a "fool hen."

All eyes were fixed on the bird. Instincts honed by hidden flushes and difficult angles tried to grasp the novelty of a target in plain view. I backed up, balancing my shotgun in my right hand, and reached for a stick. "I'm going to throw this, guys—be ready." There were affirmative nods all around.

The stick arched in the air, bounced off the tree, and fell to the ground. The grouse did not move. Never taking my eye off the bird, I found a second stick. "Here comes another one!" It struck the limb, causing the grouse to move one of its feet. One of my buddies started to chuckle lightly.

"Let me try," he said. He found a broken branch, busted it a second time to make a more compact missile, and hurled it at the living weather vane. It struck the stub, bounced off the tree, and twirled into the woods. The grouse didn't even turn its head.

I set my gun on the ground. "That's three sticks; I'm going to keep track. You cover it, and I'll throw until it flies."

I find this number incomprehensible now, but after *thirty-seven* throws the bird was still sitting on the same limb. I hit it, directly, four times. It would duck some throws, and move out of the way of others. I ran out of sticks. One of the designated "shooters" was packing his pipe, both dogs were lying on the ground, and the other man was as interested as a big-league hitting champion getting four pitch-outs.

I had to do something.

"POW!" The shot charge blew the grouse off the limb and bounced it against the tree, from which it fell in a heap to the dogs.

"Well, hell, I could've done that," said my formerly in-different friend.

"No," I responded, "this is my covert and these birds have a reputation to uphold. Let's go grouse hunting."

I felt a tap on my shoulder. My other companion held out the fool hen by one toe. "Your bird, sir—nice shot," he said, his eyes brimming with merry laughter as he strolled down the trail to the intersection.

There is a road system in the Olson Brothers. Judging from the depth of the ruts and the space between the trees it has been here a long time. Shortly after the Snow Plow was clear-cut the same company had a contract to fell some of the big white pines. In the process, they cleared a second opening along the trail and extended its far edge to connect with the black spruce bog I had to hop across to reach the high ground.

They created a wonderful corridor of scattered poplar sap-lings, young alders, and all sorts of woody trash. It is just the spot for grouse that have flown the pressure nearby. The woodcock are always here.

In some years it is too wet to walk, and in others the lush ground grows a small three-leaved plant in great profusion. I often open the crop of a fresh kill and examine the con-tents for some idea of what the birds are preferring that day. If I find the little green leaf, I come here. I don't know its scientific name, but I am also short on the names of fine wines and French cuisine. As the Incas told the Spaniards about gold, "I don't know what you call it, I just know where to find it."

I have had many experiences in this narrow place. I can recall a long litany of great red-tailed birds rising before points. By far the most memorable occasion, however, was just last year. I had Spence Turner's son with me, after dad had complained of sore knees and the desire for rest (and the pursuit of his sport of woodcocking). A grouse was pointed, and then, to escape its four-legged predator, it lifted up into a whippy sapling, bobbing up and down like an oversize Christmas ornament.

I called the young man over, stopped him with a gesture, and indicated that he should walk forward. The bird was just about head high, and only twenty-five or so yards in front of him. I think the dog's point turned the lad's attention downward, for the dog had relocated after the flush and was staunch on the scent.

The young man walked forward, closer and closer, bringing his gun up to the ready and watching for the grouse to burst up from the ground. All this time it was bobbing in the air at head level. He may have caught the movement at the last instant, but I don't think he will ever have a more dramatic flush. The powerful wings whirred air into his face and the grouse was gone. His first shot went off straight up in the air. The second saluted the takeoff.

He turned back to me, wanting to explain, I suppose. I wasn't there to see it. I was on my hands and knees, then rolling on my side, unable to give either sympathy or support. It's probably a good thing his gun was empty.

Chapter 16

In Green Pastures

If he had any idea of competing in the world, he had forgotten it. He was a ne'er-do-well, living in the grass on the side of the road with his goats. He had been left nothing except his dim brain, and this place. At night he would bring his goats inside his square log room, and they would keep each other warm. Today social workers would seek him out and appoint a bureaucrat to guide him. His goats would be sold, and he would be placed in a group home. If there were no planned activities he might be allowed to roam Main Street and smoke his cigarettes in peace. Maybe once a week he could go into the bakery, buy a bag of day-old doughnuts, and eat them all.

He had no social worker. Just two Norwegian bachelor farmers, Frank and Walt. They would stop by about once a week to bring him any mail, a few eggs, tobacco, or items that they saw he needed. If he wanted anything else he walked to town—down the hill, along the wide green trail, and across the field. One day he did not get up from under the hay piled in his room. It was cold; he got sick, and died. His neighbors took care of the burial. The land forfeited for unpaid taxes and Frank bought it from the county. Only the bottom four logs of the cabin remained, along with a heap of trash in the corner.

The Green Trail starts at the edge of Frank's alfalfa pasture, right under a tall white pine. It climbs the goatherd's hill, wide and clean, until the top. There it turns sharply right to form a corner around the old log ruins and continues straight, wide and mowed, to the Green Field. This is Frank's final pasture. It forms the other side of the hill and flows down into the low land of Rice Lake.

If there is a spiritual place in the Olson Brothers covert it is here. The long green trail leading uphill is the ascending staircase of a cathedral. The log ruin is the atrium, the open green carpet of the field road a great hall that could hold a thousand parishioners under its vaulted maple limbs. Artists and architects could labor for years and never produce a place as beautiful. Although he will never know it, the results of the simple daily efforts of a goatherd and his animals have figured largely in my life here.

A certain well-known wildlife artist likes to paint grouse flying in the wide open among birch trees. There are two things wrong. Grouse are never in the wide open and seldom among birch trees. I suspect he does this because the dark areas where the branches attach to the tree trunks can be shaped like little grouse silhouettes. No one can paint a real grouse flush. There wouldn't be much intricate detail in a grayish blur.

That is the problem with the Green Trail. It looks like the kind of woods path an artist paints. It is wide, and carpeted with short-cropped green clover. Tall hardwood trees stand on both sides of a mixture of maple, poplar, and birch, with some spruce thrown in for texture. There are no doghair poplar walls nearby. The trail flows to the Green Field like the middle aisle of a church. It is hard to take it seriously as grouse cover, but history says it shines.

A grouse covey isn't organized, like quail. That's probably a lucky thing, because the sound and fury of twelve grouse rising up at one time in a dozen different directions could unsettle a man's natural functions. My dark-haired bride was a frequent companion in the early years of the Olson explorations. I had acquired a 20-gauge Ruger shotgun for her, and while she had demonstrated that it was lethal on red squirrels and garden rabbits she had never killed a game bird. About a half-hour earlier I had stepped out on the trail ahead of her. In the middle of it stood a grouse. I was excited at the prospect of her taking her first bird, so with a loud whisper I tried to get her attention. It didn't work. The day and the leaves were too beautiful.

I went back into the brush and took her by the elbow. She was smoothing out the faces of a handful of maple leaves, balancing her shotgun in the crook of her elbow, and admiring the texture of red and gold on their surfaces.

"Cheryl!" I said. "There's a grouse on the trail right over there. C'mon, you can get a chance at it!"

She looked at me for the briefest moment as if I had lost my mind. Then, it dawned on her: We were hunting.

"Oh!" she responded. "Okay, just a second." She gave me her shotgun and opened the top flap on her jacket pocket. The stack of leaves was carefully slipped inside. "There, I'm ready."

The bird was gone, of course. Dixie had come out on the road and, seeing no one in the way, had flushed herself a reward for thirty minutes of fruitless work.

It was an in-between year. The grouse numbers were neither low nor high. The birds were coming at the rate of about two per hour, and we were due. I figured we were going to walk for another long stretch without a flush. I was wrong.

We walked up the hill, side by side, enjoying the contrast of bright summer-green clover against the yellow poplar leaves. When we reached the corner, I stopped to point out the old log walls of the goatherd's cabin. At that moment Dixie flushed two grouse from the weeds on the other side of the trail.

I killed the first one and missed the second. The dead bird fell almost straight back into the place where it had started. Three more grouse roared out.

As I tugged another shell out of my cartridge loops I glanced over to see if Cheryl was ready to shoot. Her mouth was open, and her shotgun hung loosely at the end of her hands.

"Shoot!" I yelled. "Shoot!"

Oh, right.

She didn't say that, but her expression did. She fired the 20-gauge twice, in quick succession. Nothing fell.

But four more grouse joined the other five that had just left. I snapped the action shut and pulled the trigger on the last of the bunch. It staggered but did not tumble, coasting instead across the trail in a long stall which carried it over the cabin ruins and down the hill.

Dixie was not done yet. "Reload!" I yelled. "Shoot!" I commanded. The final three of the group whirred up and banked away one after the other.

Oh, yeah...and then..."Oh, well."

Cheryl pushed the top lever over and bent the gun open. Two yellow hulls streaked out over her shoulder. "Wow, that was incredible. We have to come back here again."

Sometimes words just pile up. About six different thoughts happen at the same time on three subjects and each seems as important to say as the other. Spit seems to replace lip movement. Body gestures resemble dance steps. The life of a bird hunter is not an easy one.

At about this time Dixie came trotting up the wide green trail with the first bird.

"Not that one, you idiot!" I said, still struggling with the overload. "Get the other one, the other one!" I wanted her to chase the second bird, the one that I had crippled. With a grand gesture of my arm and a loud "Back, dammit, back!" I walked quickly into the brush behind the cabin and started downhill in pursuit of the bird's flight line.

She was a tolerant dog, in her obliging fashion. She quit what she was doing and started after me. About ten minutes later, after a useless search, it occurred to me that two things were missing: my bride, and the first bird.

I called Dixie over. I explained in long and loud terms all the ways that she had failed me. She had lost the first bird, failed to find the second one, and so on. Dixie was a great dog. She accepted all the blame, knew that she should have caught all twelve of the grouse whether shot or not, delivered each to hand, and reloaded all the guns.

There was nothing left to say. Two sad bird hunters walked out to the cabin ruins.

"What's the matter with you?" Cheryl asked.

"Well, for starters, I lost the second bird because Dixie didn't mark it down. Then she lost the first one because I called her over to find the second." I took a breath.

"Ted," she said in her quiet, firm voice (the one I have since heard in connection with child instruction), "Dixie put your first bird down in the middle of the trail." She pointed with her finger. "It's right there. Honestly, you are so intense!"

I had another one of those overload attacks, remorse on top of remorse. But I was able to form a quick comeback.

"Oh," I said.

I am a fortunate man. I have been blessed with smart females.

There is an old story often told in connection with getting what you pray for. A bird hunter once prayed for God to give him patience. God answered his prayers: He gave him a bad bird dog. I like to tell that one because it reminds me of Salty. The little English setter was hopeless for three long years until she decided that was time enough. She put away her toys and whimsies and, without a backward glance, gave me eight years of skillful bird craft. She pointed grouse, either singly or in coveys, over two thousand times. And woodcock at least as often. Of all the places we hunted, the Olson Brothers' Green Trail is where I see her when I think of her beauty.

A small point of high grass and small bushes sticks out into the long green-carpeted hallway. It is about one hundred yards from the cabin ruins. I have never found any particular herb or berry in this spot. It just seems to be the kind of place where a grouse likes to hang out. Salty knew this. In her early years she would drop her head and clamp her ears tight, pouring speed into her wiry body. No whistle could stop her from busting the bird and she would leap up after it in the same way a terrier chases a squirrel. She did this until one Sunday in November when the wind blew cool and steady from the northwest and she was old enough to listen to her ancestors. The headlong puppy charge was gone. In its place came her trademark: a smooth-flowing gait rocking back and forth like the pace of a fine riding horse instead of a cutting pony.

It is an intoxicating power to send a fast and fiery pointing dog on a long cast. But grouse hunting is not field trialing, and a grouse is not a planted quail. A grouse hunter sees a point in the open about as often as he sees a bird flying in the open. Which is to say, so seldom that it is stunning to the senses. Salty flowed into the breeze, caught the long tendril of grouse scent, slowed to a walk, stopped, crept forward two or three steps, testing the strength of the mark, and then locked every fiber of her being into a point.

A calendar with such a picture on its monthly cover would be scoffed at as romantic nonsense. The scene was too posed to be real. I don't remember if I killed that particular bird.

I just remember Salty as being perfect, and I still see her just that way whenever I stand at the cabin ruins and look down the trail.

I remember a shot there too. It was over Salty's point, but this time I came seeking the moment and the bird that I knew would be waiting.

I haven't been everywhere in the world. Just a few places— some nice, some not so pleasant. Most of the time guns have been around. The best shooter I ever saw was a common man to look at. No racy mustache, no dueling scar, and the plainest clothing you ever saw. But in his hands was an uncommon gun. It marked him as someone to be reckoned with. It was a Remington Model 1100 skeet gun, on the outside. The stock was taped on the top with several layers of moleskin to raise the comb. The pad had been extended with two black rubber spacers. At the end of the barrel was the knurled end of a competition choke tube. The breech was worn and the action clattered like bad false teeth. But in his hands it was a Stradivarius.

The trap boy came up from the first set of sporting-clay butts with this young man in tow. The two of them came over to my team of four. We were stretched out under a little tree in a relaxed fashion and, I guess, looked more congenial than some other squinty-eyed teams.

"Excuse me," the trapper said. "This guy just shot a perfect score on the first fifty. I scored it, but it looks to me like he might run them all. Will one of you take it from here? I don't want anyone to say I blinked for a big tip."

"Sure," I said. "Give me the clipboard; he can't embarrass us, we're beyond redemption."

The young man smoked those clays. He didn't chip them; he turned each saucer into dust. "What choke was he using?" one of the other team members asked me later.

"What difference does it make?" I responded. "He centered every shot." Except for two. He got 98 out of 100.

A common man, an uncommon gun.

The common denominator in my part of Vietnam was red mud. Even the puddles were the consistency and color of barn paint. My little family of medics was spread out among three combat units and once a month or so our battalion surgeon would stop by for a visit. He came down the stairs of my medical aide bunker and pulled a crate over to the litter that I had stretched between two sandbag walls. I was stitching up a soldier's cut leg, standing in about three inches of squishy red Jell-O. Mud—some of it dried, most of it not quite—was on everything. The only clean things were the cut, my surgical gloves and tools, and my M-16, hanging on the wall next to the stretcher. The patient sat stoically, smoking a cigarette, and when I was done he grunted appreciatively and slid off the litter.

"Lundy," the surgeon said, "your mother would be proud of that seam work. And that rifle is a work of art also."

In the common world of weapons and red mud it was as clean and oiled as a bathed baby.

The fraternity of bird hunters covers a broad class of humans. Like soldiers, we all look the same to the unpracticed eye. One vest looks like another, and boots are boots unless the eyes are looking for clues to the man inside. I look at the gun first. In a shooting man's world it is the thing that matters most.

Is the gun some factory marketing team's idea of what the well-clad grouse hunter ought to be carrying? Or is it like the well-worn 20-gauge automatic I once saw in the hands of a bib-overalled country boy?

Our equipment speaks words. I was resting on a log a few years ago in a cover that was so remote and private that I had never met another hunter in its borders. I had decided to wait. The noisy progress of some people was heading my way. In a few short minutes the leader of the group stepped out on the trail. Seeing me, he walked over to chat. I relaxed immediately. He had on knee-high rubber boots and was carrying a bolt-action shotgun. His companions soon stepped out in stiff new vests and long-barreled duck guns. We parted on good terms and I never saw him again, nor did I expect to. By the time he and his friends made it out of that place they would have blisters, sore arms, and a long tale about the trials of partridge hunting.

The gun that I brought for my moment on the Green Trail was the culmination of a long search, several trades, and some good luck. It was my declaration of the uncommon gun. The calling card that bespoke a seasoned bird hunter.

Soldiers wear medals and ribbons. Lawyers are required, by court rule, to be dressed in "suitable attire." Yet no strip of cloth performs the work. These are items of image. A recognition of the respect that is due. It is the tool that shows the man. A woodcutter with an eighth-grade education can look at your chain saw and know all he needs to know about your ability.

I knew what I wanted. A fine old bird gun. A 20-gauge side-by-side double with a straight-hand stock, double triggers, a splinter fore-end, and long, slim barrels. The gun had been in my mind for a long time. It couldn't be new. I wanted a classic gun. The kind by which others are measured. I wanted an English gun.

I needed a lot of luck to get one. The American taste for Belgian Browning shotguns closed the deal. A few years before this day I admired two Superposed Brownings owned by a client of mine. I was being polite, in part, because I knew that this particular brand, while being well made, was ill fitted to me. The owner died, and his widow called me shortly after and asked if I would like to buy them. I was able to buy them both for a reasonable price, but more important, they came complete with box, warranty cards, and even the original bill of sale. I kept them for a couple more years and confirmed my suspicion that with either gun it would take me two shells to hit my foot.

I seem to end up buying guns in the spring. There is no logical explanation for this, but timing is everything in a quest for the ultimate gun. A call to Griffin and Howe, the long-established dealers in New York, proved the theory. The Browning guns were very desirable to their clientele. Even better, a Westley Richards 20-bore that fit my dream specifications had just that very day found its way out of their shop and onto the sales floor. The trade was made, and with a little— but not very much—more cash the gun came into my hands.

A gun box, newly arrived, is as inviting to me as a front-opening bra. I was not disappointed. The stock was a glorious piece of walnut, the barrels newly blacked and shining, and the boxlock metal had just the right amount of engraving. It wasn't showy; it oozed style and class. The breech parts were old; the dealer placed its original manufacture at around the turn of the century. The barrels had been reproofed for modern loads and were built by F. Beesley (from Purdey's) for some previous owner. I had, in my hands, a representation of the English gun from a variety of high-quality makers.

It was wonderful to carry. At five pounds four ounces it snapped into place like a whip and smoked clay pigeons without effort. However, the test of a new gun is also its curse. It met all my criteria, for its beauty spoke volumes. But I had not killed a bird with it.

I opened the season that year with my old friends, the 12-bore Parker and the Model 31 pump. I wanted to wait until the foliage thinned out. Three weekends went by until I could no longer stand the suspense. One quiet sunny evening after work I picked the little gun out of the case, loaded it and my setter Salty into my old Kamikaze, and went to the Olson Brothers. I had an appointment on the Green Trail, just down from the log ruins at the point where the weeds come out of the woods, to make a perfect memory for a grouse gun.

I parked in my usual stopping place and the attendant woodcock was there to receive its traditional point. I was not going to let a mudbat be the first kill of my fine old bird gun. We worked the hogback ridge, raising two more woodcock and only one grouse. It flushed wild without even a bad opportunity, let alone a good chance. I didn't linger long in my search. The only grouse appropriate for the first bird was the Green Trail partridge. If it was lingering in the usual haunts I would have a wide-open cover-girl point and as clear a shot as a grouse ever gives.

The little Westley 20-gauge had one clear shortcoming. It did not swing smoothly. A light gun has no inertia and is too easy to stop when the trigger-finger bears down. I hoped for a going-away inside angle. I could see it in my mind. The wiry setter on point in the early twilight glowing white against the green clover, the bird rising up and then banking to one side or the other. The shot would take it between the wide trunks of the trail poplars. It would fall straight down out of a drifting cloud of gray feathers.

I wear shooting gloves, thin buckskin, fitted tight to my hands, all the time. I looked down at my hands, gripped around the gun's slim wrist and forearm. The tops of the gloves were already wet with nervous perspiration. We reached the summit of the Green Trail hill and turned the corner. Salty moved ahead, not running, just floating along the ground waiting for the thin vapor trail of the grouse to hit her nose. She slowed, and stopped. I walked quickly to close the distance. It was not yet a solid point, but she had an inkling and was sorting out its message. She took a few more steps and then leaned forward. Half of my dream was coming true. The point was developing right where I had planned it. Then, in true grouse-hunting fashion, everything changed.

Salty dropped her head, took two quick hops over to the cluster of weeds, wagged her tail furiously, and turned. The bird had moved. She trailed it briefly in the roadside grass, came out, crossed the trail, and locked down, solid on scent and sight, locating the grouse in a copse of spruce trees—dark, dense, and green. I was out of position and out of luck. The bird was sure to flush on the opposite side of the pines and coast downhill out of sight.

I must have been holding my breath, for the air ran out of me then like a deflating balloon.

"Damn, I really wanted that shot!"

In the very next instant the grouse flushed in the pines—I heard it go. My little 20-gauge was up and mounted, with the long, slim barrels following the sound. I thought there might be a flicker of wings or a brief glimpse through the understory. I was wrong. The grouse came out of the spruce trees at full speed, level, and about halfway between the ground and the evening sky. It was a wide-open right-to-left shot.

My first thought was "I'll never catch up!" It was a hard-left screamer, the kind of chance professional trap shooters will pass up. I swung the lightweight double, sweeping from behind and passing through the gray-brown blur. I recall its wings being swept back, its head and neck seeming twice as long, like the blade end of an arrow. I pressed the trigger and kept my left arm moving. If I didn't hit it, at least I was waving good-bye.

Its head snapped back and its legs dropped; the bird turned half over, not flying, just following gravity. It was no longer supersonic. It was mine.

I was prepared to be philosophical, even sportsmanlike. You know, that English thing—"Bad shot, old chap, but good form." It wasn't necessary. I could immerse myself in immaturity and illegal end-zone demonstrations. Details of this sort of self-indulgence are ugly, but I can tell you that I did not spike the gun or the bird. I did pick the dog up and give her a hug. She shook it off and went looking for another grouse.

We found one, too. I killed a second bird on the way back to the car. I keep a diary and I wrote that down, but it was a short subject next to the main feature.

Carrying on about the ownership of a fine gun smacks of elitism or even snobbery. I don't consider it either of these things. It is more in the nature of philosophy. I can best explain it through the story of a young apprentice to a Chinese jade merchant. He asked his master to teach him how to select the finest jade from other rough gems. The merchant told him to sit before him. He handed the young man stones as he told him stories of philosophy, theory, and wisdom. After weeks of handling different stones and listening to the old man, the apprentice was stopped in the middle of the merchant's discourse.

"What stone do you have in your hand?" the old man asked.

The boy answered without hesitation: "Jade," he said.

A fine gun is like that. Other shotguns will work, some may be more beautiful, but a fine gun feels like something more than its parts.

I, however, don't always feel so centered. Some days the weather keeps the Westley Richards at home. On other days I have used it poorly, convincing myself that the magic is gone. Then I reach for my Parker 12-bore or the Model 31 pump. Shel Silverstein once wrote that after a steady diet of champagne and brandy, beans taste fine.

They work pretty well too. I shot my first double on a two-bird rise down where the Green Field meets the old Rice Lake ice heave.

Back when there was water in the lake, the spring winds piled ice up on the south shore. The big jagged cakes pushed a berm of sand up along the edge. It became a treeline rising above the field. Salty made a point on the top of the sand ridge, facing out into the heavy brush and swamp grass. I whistled to my companions, and gestured with my hand, indicating the dog's location. They waved me on ahead.

I was about halfway up the side, just able to see over the top, when the two birds flushed straight up, side by side. The bird on the left kept going straight. Its companion held back slightly and banked to the right, crossing behind the first. I swung the Parker on the first, blotted it out, and pressed the trigger. Dixie was alongside me, so I didn't even wait to see the results of the shot. The second grouse was curling off to my left.

The Parker is, relatively speaking, a heavy gun. After the first shot it moved, almost by itself, to the left and down. The second grouse was right in front of the barrels. I pressed the back trigger and it fell.

I never took my eyes off the spot and neither did Salty. She dove into the tall grass and in a moment was knocking the stems back and forth with her tail, standing happily over the dead bird while her friend Dixie came trotting up with the first grouse.

I sat down. Dixie gave me her bird and went over to pick up the other one. She brought it back and I held them up in one hand.

I heard a camera shutter click. One benefit of hunting with outdoor writers is the constant presence of the photographic record. Publishers pay money for pictures. They won't buy this one; it's on my wall.

I have another picture from the Green Field. It is in my mind. The great gray bird. I worked on his demise for two years. He owned the sand ridge and took a lot of pleasure in fooling me. He was as predictable as the Green Trail partridge but very crafty. His escape was always well planned.

There was a single dense gray dogwood bush growing on the field side of the berm. The grouse spent most of his time under it and made an effort to leave his scent on the damp earth. He could hear the dogs. Even Salty, as cunning as she was about the wiles of the grouse, could not help stopping for a point on the wrong side of the ridge.

As soon as her bell was silent, he would flush away, having run to the other side of the sand berm and out into the brushy lake bed.

I didn't get him on my own. It took team work. I told my companion about the dogwood bush and directed him to take his dog, a small, busy Brittany spaniel, to the far left of the mark. Then I would follow my usual pattern of approach. The Brittany would scramble over the hump and out into the heavy cover and quarter back to the far side of the berm. If the Great Gray One was home and up to his tricks, he would trot over the top and be met with a black-and-white surprise.

He almost got away. The Brittany flushed him earlier than we planned. He had run over the top, but then scurried along the other side away from the marking bush. My companion was caught with his back turned and got off a quick snapshot.

I can see the bird now, flying back along the ridge, tail spread wide and gray against the sky. I had the Model 31 that day, waiting, as if I had decoys, until he was just perfect. Then, with one swift move and shot, he fell into the swamp grass.

Sometimes I wish bird hunting was like other sports. Make a nice play and throw the ball back to do it all over. It is that philosophy thing sneaking in again. I start thinking about what I am doing and hoping it is more than the sum of its parts.

Chapter 17

In the Public Domain

I call it the West Side. I have hunted the Olson Brothers' cover for many years but I have never gone there first. Maybe it's because I always end up parking with the Leonard Woodcock, Yellow Bowl, and Green Trail covers in front of me. I never seem to get around to it. A man and a dog only have just so much energy. On the other hand, if there were a lot of birds over on the West Side the principle of effort and reward would eventually wear down my resolve to stay clear of the place.

It is big, well over eight hundred acres. It should be stiff with grouse, for it has had the benefit of all the theories of wildlife management. It has been clear-cut, in textbook blocks, for well over fifteen years. The creek seepage that feeds the waters of Rice Lake runs along its north side, providing a lush source of nutrient. On the south it rises and falls in hills and ridges, furnishing the shade and variety that grouse love. It isn't a question of excess hunting pressure either; private holdings bar the entry of road hunters.

So why is it that with all this help a tract perfectly designed by knowledgeable state technicians has fewer birds than private covers formed without a thought toward wildlife?

I don't know.

The question has come up more than once. Every time I think about it, I am sitting on a log at the very bitter end of a state tract with the dogs sleeping at my feet and my right leg cramping in anticipation of an empty walk back to the car.

Screwed again.

I am going to put a written note in my pocket. It will say: "Ted, going to hunt the West Side? Don't do it!"

The human mind is naturally optimistic, otherwise how could we have come so far? It focuses upon and strives to remember only the good things that have happened. The ancient caveman remembers the fine taste of a woolly-mammoth steak and resolves to go out and get one. Upon arriving he looks at the towering target and the club in his hand and recalls why it is not a steady staple in his diet. The West Side is more subtle. It doesn't tower. It looks wonderful, open, inviting, undulating in sensuous curves. The mind says, "It's perfect." The memory forgets.

If the memory does work, it recalls things like Ra-a-a-y Charles. That is the name of a small tongue of poplar trees, alders, hazel brush, and gray dogwood on the farthest border of the West Side (naturally). This little slice of heaven lies right up against the county road, separating it from a grass pasture. My Missouri friends found it. I recall the three of them sitting in the sunlit glade catching their collective breaths after an unrewarding but stirring trek through the clear-cut.

"You ever been over there?" one of them asked, gesturing toward the road.

"Sure," I answered, "we drove down it this morning."

"No, I mean in that little strip of woods between here and there."

"No," I responded. "I never have."

"Looks like a good spot for woodcock," he answered.

Another voice drawled out of the shade: "Thas why he niver has."

They crossed the grass pasture, tugging me along. It wasn't a good spot for woodcock.

It was a great spot!

It is called a "fall" of woodcock if a flock of the little fellows lands in one spot. Ra-a-a-y Charles had woodcock to spare, to mortgage, to rent, to give to the poor. The little Brittany spaniels simply stepped from point into point. It was not uncommon for one of them to point a bird while returning with a dead one. My little white setter Salty pointed while balancing on a log! I saw Mike McIntosh, who was one of those three men, kill a woodcock going straight away from his left, then pivot 180 degrees and kill a second straight-away on his right. Joel Vance, another of the men, grassed four doodles before his dogs picked up the first one.

We took almost a four-man limit, calling things to a halt to find the downed birds. The simplest thing to do was to back out into the field and let the dogs pick up. After every bird was accounted for, it was the opinion of the committee that the place should have a name. Blues music is a big part of their civilian lives. I don't have much knowledge of it myself, living in northern Minnesota and all, but I thought "Whoopy John" would be good. They gave it their own name. Thereafter whenever any one of them would say "We gonna go see Ra-a-a-y Charles!" I knew where we were headed.

It is also evidence of my mystery. Ra-a-a-y Charles is on private land, adjacent to hundreds of acres of public management.

Maybe that's the clue: hundreds of acres and management. It's too big and it's all the same. I have the same problem with fishing big lakes. Everything I seek—in addition to good companionship, the chance to get out, etc.—is somewhere under all that sameness.

At least if the sameness were water it would be a lot easier to get around. In a state clear-cut there is a trail and then there is not-a-trail. The trail takes up a twelve-foot ribbon of open space, generally ending at a log landing. You either walk back the way you came or dive into the not-a-trail.

Before the advent of mechanized logging, trees were cut down by hand, topped and limbed in place. Then the log was dragged by horse or machine to the landing, where it was cut into eight-foot bolts and stacked. Some trees got left behind with the tops and limbs of those hauled away. When the saplings sprouted up around the stump they wove into and around the mess. These clear-cuts were impenetrable. They had one thing in their favor, however: the handcutting made them small and a man could walk around the perimeter. I am speaking of openings made by the pulp cutters, the scavengers of the wood industry, eking out a living on paper-company contracts and firewood supply.

They left the woods in this condition because they didn't have the time, or the inclination, to tidy up. At fifty cents a cord, whiners like me could be damned. My favorite acquaintance among them was a hardy Finn who stopped by my office one day to discuss a land transfer to his son. After we filled in the deed and discussed the land description, he talked a little about his life.

He could cut and haul three loads a day—more if he had a good man on the other end of the saw handle. The eight-foot logs, usually poplar, were loaded onto his truck, a single-axle Chevrolet, in the green. These were driven to town ,where he would unload them, by himself, one log under each arm. I thought he was bragging a bit, but my dad saw him do it.

"He would pull two logs off the back of the truck. Then by stepping between them and catching each around the middle, he would balance the bolts, tuck his arms up into his ribs, and walk to the customer's coal chute. One end was stuck into the opening and pushed forward until it would disappear. Then he would poke the other log down. At that time, burning green wood and coal was a common way to get more heat out of less fuel."

He still looked fit even as an old man. His eyes would sparkle and the black burned stub of a pipe would bounce as he described his history.

"Yah, I tell yu, vhen ve had the big saw it vas yust okay. But vhen ve got dah Svede saw I thot I culd cut dah whole voods down! Und den ve got the chain saw. Oh my, dat vas swell!"

Modern progress is paved with paperwork. The demand for pulpwood to produce more of that paving outstripped the old Finn's ability to cut it; fuel oil and old age took care of the rest. Rubber-tired skidders became commonplace. Now the work is performed in air-conditioned or heated cabs atop hydraulic snippers and machines that limb the whole tree, cut it, and stack the finished product on semitrailers.

Curiously enough, though life got easier for the logger, it got tougher for the bird hunter. A fresh clear-cut is easy to walk through. The stumps are cut down almost to ground level; the limbs and tops are stacked in piles at the log landing. The area is huge, but the easy walking only lasts about one year. Then the hairbrush-thick poplar saplings take over.

I hunted the West Side before its management days. The poplar was old, thirty to thirty-five years, but nicely organized by two-rut, grass-centered trails. It was my late-season storehouse. When the frost had taken down the other food, the grouse would gather in the big poplar to trim the buds. The shooting was open and exciting, for the birds seemed to sense their vulnerability. A modified choke was the rule. It was the mother lode for all dodge-behind-the-tree stories.

The edge of my old poplar grove started where a tall grove of big red pines still stands. I had been away from the place for all of the bird season. The farm side of the Olson Brothers was too good to pass up and produced enough birds each time. There had been no need to walk west. A light snow had reminded me of those old poplars, and I walked directly through the red pine looking forward to some fast action.

The impact of so much open space was as stunning as if there had been a loud explosion. It wasn't about what was there; it was about what was missing. Like the old story about the guy who slept next to the railroad tracks. One day the train didn't come on time and he jumped up and said, "What was that?"

It was over. From the red pines all the way to Ra-a-a-y Charles, it looked like the attack of the alien tree-suckers. I tried to put a good spin on it. In a few years, maybe ten years, I mused, the birds would be back. It would make good brood cover. Think of the future.

Those ten years, plus a few more, are now past. I know that it is possible to move through this geographic area. It is also possible to pull a comb through tangled hair. You get the same results: a sore spot. My old trails, which met one another and divided the country into islands of habitat, are now replaced by dead-end hallways. The walls of these corridors are poplar saplings about twenty to the square foot.

I am back to fishing in big water. I know the game is in here, but where? As I said before, a grouse is a creature of edges. I have no openings. I am a grouse hunter, thus an incurable optimist. But if an optimist is a person who digs through piles of horse manure knowing that a pony must be in there somewhere, I am coming up with only horse manure.

I believe it is a question of technique. The wildlife manager in this county just happens to also be the most successful grouse hunter I have ever known. He is also the most successful grouse hunter you have ever known. If success is going to be measured by birds brought to bag I can tell you that I killed a hundred and one grouse in my best year. He did better than that by almost half again. On an annual, and anonymous, survey of grouse hunters nationwide, he is number one. We are not talking about a beergut braggart here. This is one of the good guys, sort of an Amish farmer in grouse-hunting clothes. He is long and lean with an incurable addiction to fine double guns. That is pretty much where it ends. No Volvo wagons, no oiled cotton coats. He doesn't care much about a good first impression, and is solitary by nature, hunting with a few select companions. I am not one of them.

He only hunts what he knows: public land. That is why I think it may be a question of technique. He does it all with a golden retriever—not a world-class pointing dog—that is a close-working extension of himself. In my finest year I had the benefit of my setter Salty, who was at the peak of her game. This guy does it on knowledge. He knows how to hunt the big sameness. He's a good public servant too, and is curious about my prejudice against the big clear-cuts. We have talked about these places. I used to doubt his reports. My disbelief was based mostly on an opinion he had. He would look me right in the eye and state:

"If you go out into those big clear-cuts in the first year, you will see that the saplings have grown big green leaves. These stay fresh and green even through several frosts. In about mid-October in the late afternoon the grouse will come out of the heavy cover to feed on these and they are as easy to shoot as sharptail."

Right. I also remember the old light-in-the-bag-for-snipe story. The worst part was that at the end of some quiet afternoons I found myself poking around new clear-cuts, after checking over my shoulder to make sure I was alone.

I suspect that he wonders about me from time to time as well. My love for private holdings is where we will remain different. I know, and he has stated, that he can't bring himself to ask permission to hunt. It is probably that old fear that we all share. The one that kept us staring at the phone when we wanted to call up the prom queen and ask her out. You know, rejection...combined with laughter. It is a valid emotion. Fear of being embarrassed has killed cowards who otherwise would have run from the enemy. In this part of Minnesota a lot of local landowners fit the mold of, "Great people once they get to know you."

Still, the wildlife manager is undeniably successful at his form of hunting. Which reminds me of a story one of my friends used to tell about his son. The boy just couldn't seem to kill a pheasant. Until he killed one his dad would only allow him to eat the legs. The seasons went by without improvement. Finally his dad asked him if he was tired of eating pheasant legs.

"Nah," the boy answered, "I learned to like 'em."

I guess if you're going to be a one-trick pony it might as well be a good one, and the public-land man is a good one. He empties a box of shells in one vest pocket, a box of shells in the other pocket, and sticks a bottle of cola and a bratwurst in his game bag. Somewhere during the day he will stop to make a fire and cook the sausage. I don't think he can walk on the top of the brush so, therefore, he must be down in the thick wildlife management that he has designed. He has his own technique and I don't have a clue how it works. But I do have a confession to make:

Last fall I walked through a new clear-cut, without a flash-light or snipe bag.

The young poplar suckers were up, and upon each one there were hung five or six big green leaves. My partner Bill Habein and I had put in a long day working our dogs through the patches and clumps of our favorite farms. We decided to finish our day trolling for grouse. It was a tract of state man-agement land and we didn't have a more pressing place to be on that late afternoon. I walked the tote road at the lead.

He and I don't hunt side by side. One leads, the other follows along some distance behind, each with his own dog. I came to the pile of tops and cut limbs. All around me the green leaves of young poplar were waving in the breeze about waist high. This kind of hunting was a standing joke between Bill and me. Sometimes I would stop to mount the gun and swing on an imaginary flush. "Write the state," he would call. "Tell them the management plan is working." This time, however, my dog was on point. A very solid point. I gestured with my hand. My partner grinned and waved it off. I shook my head to say, "No, I am not kidding." Before he could cover the distance between us, a grouse flushed, clearing the waist-high leaftops, and died instantly for its error. A second bird, to the right of the first, flushed behind it. I missed that one. The old Parker does not have ejectors, but if the shooting has not fouled up the chambers too badly I can open the gun, spin it in my hands, and throw out the fired shells. It had been a quiet day, so in a short three seconds I reloaded— just in time to knock down a third grouse that flushed straight away on my left.

By this time Bill was by my side. He shot into his own double rise, killing one and missing the other.

We looked at each other and grinned.

"My lips are sealed," I said.

"This never happened," he replied.

Until we learn the technique, I don't want the state to know that their management theories might be working.

Chapter 18

The Wagon Wheel

Places are sometimes described by things that are gone. In the summers between my law school years I worked as an over-the-road salesman for a biscuit company. One day my travels took me to a town called Pine Island. That is not an unusual name, unless the town is in southern Minnesota, where there are no pines. I probably would have passed up an inquiry about the name, except a couple other things had attracted my attention. The store clerk was bright and pretty, and travelers were allowed to park in the middle of the street.

The pretty clerk had no explanation for the city parking. But I learned three things: customers were more important than salesmen; there was no island; and there were no pines.

There was, however, a wagon wheel. Not in Pine Island, but on the county highway at a driveway next to forty acres of state land. It's gone now, along with the mail box it supported, but not before the old wooden wheel gave its name to the adjacent grouse and woodcock cover.

A tall Norway pine, too young to cut at the time when the timber companies came through, still stands, its top blasted off by lightning. A limb grows out of the north side at the very tip, extending its branches toward the road and forming a bushy green hand that seems to gesture to me in an open-palmed fashion saying: "C'mon in, the water's fine."

This is woodcock country. If the sun is low in the sky, a bird hunter can see the sparkle of stagnant coffee-colored pools under the grass and alders. Like the wheel after which it was named, the place has spokes of dry land running between the sinkholes. And like the old story, the trick to walking on water is to know where the rocks are.

No game management has been imposed upon its face. It is a stew of habitat, without any commercial value. The dry ridges support poplar, but not enough to cut. The pine tree islands have been left alone for the same reason. If hazel brush had any market price, the Wagon Wheel would be the mother lode. For reasons that are a mystery to me (since I am not a student of the species) it is also Palm Beach to migrating woodcock.

It is a singular entity, inhospitable and difficult. A half-day in this environment will leave the shooter wet to his knees, and cut in a dozen places. The old alder limbs lie on top of previous generations, dense and unyielding, all hidden in tall grass. Under it all, the earth has formed itself in swampgrass humps, some solid and others floating, which invite a tentative step and then collapse under a full stride. The dry land fingers bristle with woolly hazel clumps. Poplar saplings are troublesome, but being whiplike they can be pushed aside. Hazel brush reaches into your pockets and intimate parts, taking hold.

When Salty was in her middle years I stopped at the Wagon Wheel for a quick turn through one of its grouse corners.

What I had in mind was a thirty-minute loop across one of the two main spokes, or fingers. It had been a warm afternoon in late September. Most of the foliage was still up, and the frost had not been strong enough to take down the grass and ferns. My old friend Dixie was retired, and her replacement, Jet, also a black Lab, was young and occupying my attention. We flushed a grouse almost right away, inside the woods' edge. There had been no point, just a lucky happenstance. The young bird rose above the dense understory and continued a straight, fast climb into the tree leaves. I swung the gun up to meet the line and followed quickly, taking the shot as if it were a trap target. Even though the bird made it into the overstory and disappeared, the cloud of copper-plated $7^1/2$s caught up and took it cleanly. Jet was inexperienced but was, and remains, a superb marking dog. She caught sight of the fall, and I had my bird.

Salty, on the other hand, was gone. I was not concerned. I could hear her bell. The sound carried well and indicated she was pushing through the other side of the ridge. Soon she would be out among the woodcock. I had my grouse, Jet had made a fine retrieve—I wanted to end it and go home.

I blew my whistle. This hunt was over. I had some evening errands; the woodcock would get along fine without me. Hunting dogs do not have an "off" switch. But Salty was not a wild child. She always came when called.

Not this time. At first I was annoyed. In my mind I was done. Mentally I was already about halfway back to the car. She, on the other hand, had fallen for the allure of the big pine. Its open green hand had drawn her in. Even worse, for me, was the almost certain fact that she was on point. She was locked as tight as a deer tick on a shaggy dog, and less easy to find.

I blew my whistle again and again, hoping to break the spell. She would not come in. I had to go out. The Wagon

Wheel is a hard hunt with the morning's first energy. It is a green hell at day's end.

Jet slinked along in my wake. I was leaving a vapor trail of mutterings. I suppose one of those beepers would have helped. But it was too late now. It was also too late for my right boot as it sank into a wet hole, running a greasy streak of black mud up my shin.

"Dammit, Salty, shake your head or something!"

Still no sound. A couple woodcock flushed up in front of my thrashing. I decided to follow their short flight. One direction was as good as another. I blew my whistle some more. Maybe if I shot into the air she would move enough to ring the bell.

No. If I did that Jet would set off in pursuit of the doodles. I just had to keep slogging and circling in wider arcs. The grass was too high and the alders too thick. A little white dog half sunk in the mud had nothing to show above the mess.

Annoyance gives way to fear. It is subtle, but before long the prickling claws of panic begin to creep up the sides of your neck and move along the cheekbones.

"Salty," I called, "come, move, do something!"

Then, I heard it. The lightest tinkle. Just a small foreign sound to my left. In a few more steps I could see a long, straight white line. It was her backbone. I sloshed a few more yards, now wet to my back pockets, and I could make out her body. She was pressed to the ground. In a few moments I was alongside her. Her ears were down, her tail was flat to the mud, she was moving her head slowly from side to side.

"What the hell?" I barked at her.

That was enough to flush a woodcock from just under her nose. Jet, now released from her following mode, scrambled around us. Four more woodcock flushed up. Salty had apparently walked into a group of the doodles and froze tight. She could hear me all the time but was unable to move. Every direction she wanted to take had a bird in the way.

"It's a good thing they don't eat dog meat," I mumbled. "Let's go home."

Can a man and a place be indistinguishable? I suspect so. Cities are sometimes named after men. There could be an Olson Brothers cover without Frank and Walt, but they are so much a part of what makes it special that I can't imagine the land without them. Uncle Willie's farm is gone now. Someone else owns it. I don't hunt there any more, partly because the birds are gone, and partly because the essence of the place is lost without Willie and Marlys Weiss. Even when the people are gone, sometimes a place retains their special presence. The Pedersen farm has had none of that family for thirty years, yet it is indelibly marked. The Wagon Wheel and Joel Vance are also as one.

Scientists speculate that all matter, from human to the subatomic to the planets, is made of honeycombs shaped in different sizes. Between the hard sides—in whatever shape— runs dark matter. It's all around us, whistling past our ears and through our atoms without sound, the stock of a cosmic soup, according to an article by James Trefil in the June 1993 issue of *Smithsonian*. Sort of the black stuff between the stars, the space between our atoms. I believe it. I have seen my friend Joel walk into the Wagon Wheel and disappear as if he merged his molecules with its organic matter.

It is the first place he hunted on the first day he came here. It is the last place he hunts, by himself, every year before he leaves. The tapestry of Joel and the Wagon Wheel are as interwoven as a handbraided rug.

Difficult, bristly, and complex, on the one hand, and generous, amusing, and infinitely varied on the other. With this much in common it is small wonder that man and place share an affinity, one for the other. The Wagon Wheel cannot be dealt with straight on; neither can Joel. They both defy classification and organization. Joel loves it for that. If three hunters line up on its south edge intending to work their way through to the highway on the north they will be separated, confounded, and turned around by bird and bush until it is every man, and every dog, for himself. It is as inscrutable as a martial arts master.

For example, in karate the best defense to a straight-in attack is to circle the thrust. In the Wagon Wheel any straight path is met by a swamphole or a hazel-brush thicket. One hunter is held up and has to walk around the obstacle. The other pushes forward unaware that his partner is turned about. He can't be seen, and we don't shout back and forth. If a grouse flushes, by accident or design, there are so many fine hiding places close by that the bird often circles and drops quickly—a classic woodcock technique that has not been lost on the birds' partridge neighbors. Joel and my other hunting companions all use pointing dogs in some configuration. Whether Brittany spaniel, English setter, or German shorthair, the breed hunts beyond the handler's boottip. This cover has no long sweeps. The hunter enters the woods, the dog surges forward, both disappear. There are no apple orchards, stone walls, or trails, just brush and birds. Lots of those pointy-nosed, chunky, worm-sucking types. It may be a mecca for the woodcock, but it is better described as a ghetto. These migrants leave their manners in Canada. They are all streetwise.

When you get down in the mud with the pigs the first thing you learn is: they like it there. It's the same with Joel. Drop the gloves, dig in, and start swinging. He hunts without the Marquis of Queensberry rules. A master of unconventional warfare, he intends to be the last man standing in the toughest place on earth.

I know when he is among the woodcock. Our mutual friend, Spence Turner, gives himself away with his signature two quick shots. Joel is a symphony. Brass horns, cymbals, and choruses in crescendos and hallelujahs. It goes like this (audio only):

Whoa! Whoa! You better whoa! BANG! Back! Get 'im. You better listen to me! Whoa! Steady, steady. BANG! Whoa! Doc get back here! Dammit, you listen to me! Good dog, good dog. No! Not there! Over there, over there! BANG! BANG! Damn dog, you listen to me! Good dog. Whoa now, steady. Oh, that damn tree!

The Wagon Wheel gives him all he can stand. It also gives him its secrets. Somewhere out there in the sparkling waters he has found the hub to its spokes. He can walk on its surface. Spence and I have talked about this while squeezing out our socks. If the three of us are going to hunt the Wagon Wheel we know that Spence and I will hunt as a pair. Joel will merge his molecules with the place and then somehow magically reappear a long ways away. You can't hunt with foxfire; it likes the swamp.

I blame it on the woodcock. I can't prove it, but I suspect that a close examination of Joel, and even Spence, for that matter, would find a hidden puncture wound. Sort of like a benign vampire bite. Once bitten, stabbed, or whatever, they are drawn into places like the Wagon Wheel seeking the source of their addiction. One can't trust a bird whose brain is in backwards. I go along with the dogs. Some won't even pick one up. My old Lab Dixie, a compulsive eater of cow manure, would retrieve the "little russet fellers" but always curled her lip in distaste. Joel and Spence, however, look upon my singular view as narrow-mindedness. If I could find the magic path to the dry land spokes, and if I moved quietly enough, I believe that I would see Joel Vance standing in a poplar vale like St. Francis of Assisi with the woodcock settling on him like little sparrows. That is not to say the Wagon Wheel has no grouse. It does, and it stores them in dry places in astonishing profusion.

There is an old black Hudson car turned upside down on the edge of the green hay pasture that borders the Wagon Wheel. I have permission to park there and hunt those portions of the bordering land that are not mowed for cattle feed. I am not sure exactly how, but Joel always disappears near the car. I think the old hulk covers a tunnel opening. I have looked it over, carefully, poking inside the open trunk, but I have found nothing. Spence and I agree, however, that this is where Joel escapes into the Wagon Wheel's dark matter.

"He's headed out into those dry land fingers," Spence said on one occasion. "We should hear him in about twenty minutes."

We looked at each other and grinned. "Whoa, Guff! Dammit, you better whoa!" we said at the same time and collapsed in laughter. Guff was Joel's dear friend and constant canine. He was also the source of loud and long sessions of unheeded dog commands. Guff knew the game and was going to do it his way. Joel knew better, and wanted to do it his way. French Brittany against tough little Irishman. They argued all the way out and all the way back, pointing, killing, and retrieving woodcock in the interim. Guff's gone now but not forgotten.

"Let's go along the swamp edge and up into the pine grove where the big Norway stands," I said. "We'll stop next to the big blowdown. Then we can work the setters into the wind until we reach the highway right-of-way. By that time Joel should be shouting and shooting, and we can pick our way through the shallow stuff and meet him."

It took us a while to reach the tall pine. The tree and its companions shaded away the dense undergrowth, providing a cool opening for a break. Salty, Jet, and I were there first. We waited and listened for our tanklike companion.

Spence is what one would politely refer to as vertically impaired. He is shorter than the surrounding brush. Even with a blaze-orange hat, he is best located by sound. In the heavy growth he is as subtle as a cannonball. He is a symphony of his own. An entire percussion section resides in his hunting vest. Old dog bells clink, shells rattle, nylon swoops against branches. It is a load that would stagger lesser men. I have accused him of carrying a spare dog in the game pocket, but he denies this. He talks to himself and his setter as he puffs along, chuckling at old jokes, directing his dogs with commands to "c'mon around."

I saw the bushes shaking by the blowdown.

"Let's go dogs! Spence is out in front of us." I walked out of the little pine park and put my back against the hazel brush, pushing it up until I could slide underneath.

"My dog is on point in here someplace," said Spence. He was facing me, the dry gray trunk of the blowdown just behind him.

"I don't hear any beeper," I responded.

"Doesn't work, but I've got another one in my pocket," he said.

"You've got a whole hardware store in your pocket." I was just getting warmed up, having been given the opportunity. "Then there's the clothing store in your game pouch."

"Now don't start with me..." He never finished. The point was right under the deadfall. A grouse flushed up less than eight feet from his head and roosted on the branch of a stunted burr oak. He raised his gun. "Where is it?"

"Right there, in that little tree." He didn't see it; instead another grouse came up out of the same dry mass of pine branches. It fell dead at his shot. Two more flew up. I killed one, he got the other. Then all the dogs joined in the madness. Points were out of the question; the birds were young and foolish and scurrying about on the ground looking for holes in the branches to fly up through.

We faced one another. Real heroes would stand back-to-back, but we are just ordinary men. I shot at the birds rising off his right shoulder and he did the same for me. We stood so close we could have loaded each other's guns. When the smoke cleared, there was still one left. It was in the little stunted burr oak right behind his head.

"Kill that one!" I nodded with my head, both hands busy trying to reload.

"Which one?"

"That one!" I bobbed my head up and down, pointing with my chin.

"Where?"

"There, right there!"

I slapped the action shut and stepped around him. At that moment it decided to go. It was the same instant that he spotted the movement.

"Jeezus!" he yelled, and cracked off his last two shots.

We turned face-to-face. "Nope, don't say anything. I'm going to think of a number," I said. "You do the same." I waited a moment. "Okay, what's your number?" I asked.

"A dozen."

"Counting that last one, I guess ten," I responded.

"How many did we get?" he asked.

"Four."

"One for each dog," he said. When Spence laughs, the first burst is just a happy open mouth and a few dry clicks. Then he takes a breath and gets into it.

Laughter is clearly the best release. Years ago Spence and I shared a similar moment out on the Green Field. Mike McIntosh hates hats. But upon our unanimous insistence he went to the local hardware store and purchased a blaze-orange item. It was a Taiwanese imitation of a poor hat. It needed to be shot. I did this, snatching it off his head and tossing it into the air. Unfortunately I only ticked the brim. Mike pointed this out to me and said it was a rude way to treat a fine chapeau. I took it from him, looked at it, and agreed that I had missed. Then I dropped it on the ground and blew it up. Spence collapsed. He fell to his knees and rolled on the ground. I am a sucker for slapstick, but Spence Turner becomes helpless. He rolls on the ground like a box turtle. That triggered my own hysteria; and Mike, watching for a moment, reached down, dusted off his hat, and placed it carefully on his head. Spence and I saw this and fell over against one another.

"I bought two," he said. "You guys are hopeless."

He was right.

We had gotten our breath, dried our eyes, and were picking up the birds when a voice called out: "What was all the shouting and shooting about?"

It was Joel. And it took another five minutes to regain control.

Joel was tolerant of our behavior. In the same manner that a museum guard at the Louvre endures a high school tour group. This place is, after all, his mile marker. He comes here every year to find out how far down the road he has traveled. Like the old bear, he has to check the claw marks on his scratching tree. He wants the land to know that he has come back and he can still whip it.

If he is with us on the last afternoon, Joel will say: "Leave me and the dogs at the Wagon Wheel; pick me up when you're done, but not before sunset." Joel is neither helpless nor frail, but as I splash the old car through the puddles and bounce across the last two potholes I always have this fear that he won't be sitting in the grass with his two Brittanies, one under each arm, when we return. That he won't stand up in a hard-earned creaky sort of way, toss his vest in the back with two or three woodcock, and sit down next to us on the seat. I want to hear him say those two all-encompassing words—"good hunt"—and then lapse into silence.

If he wasn't there I couldn't do anything about it. He and the Wagon Wheel would be one. I don't think he would mind all that much.

Chapter 19
A Square Mile

There is a sign on the wall of the local liquor store that reads: "No Offensive Profanity Allowed." I appreciate the latitude. It allows rough edges. The people that settled my county were lumberjacks, trappers, and other half-settled types. Their descendants are still here. I have made part of my legal reputation defending fistfights and other forms of violent recreation. The same guy who printed the sign decided to promote a sticky but powerful liquid called Yukon Jack. It was on special that night, which is to say it was cheaper than a shot and a beer. One thing led to another and some of it got spilled inside the piano when the player wouldn't quit repeating the only tune he knew: "Anchors Aweigh." One wouldn't think that a patriotic theme could cause such a commotion. I told the judge that the piano player must have been trying to reach his glass and that was how he had ended up inside the piano. The mayor said no more specials. I think that's wrong because half the piano keys don't work anymore, and it was the tune that caused the problem in the first place.

Anyway, down in the agricultural part of Minnesota the corners are all square, the fences straight, and the people in bed by nine. A lawyer could starve down there. If this land had been less tough and Mother Nature's bosom a little softer, the hills would be clear of thick bristly places, and the streams tiled and drained. Up here the land fought back after the timber companies came through. It raised rock to bend the plows, and jack pine to fill the fields that couldn't be tilled. Whenever the farmer was too tired or too broke to fight, the poplar pressed against his field edges. The purebred man gathered his family and moved south. The half-settled man took a tip from the coyote and diversified. He grew a little corn, raised a few cattle, hunted the deer, and shot the birds. Some pieces of land couldn't be settled. Some men can't be tamed. It's a good thing. I can make a living defending the wild side of men and hunting the hard ground.

It says in Genesis that on the seventh day God rested. I know where he parked his glacier when he took a break. On one side he left the floodplain of Wood Row Creek, on the other side the valley of Goblin Creek. The parking place is the one square mile of rocks and debris that flowed out to form the Maple Hills.

They are easy to find. The Pedersen farm road is on one side, the Olson Brothers' road across the top, and the county road down the other side. At the bottom lie the remains of the old township cartway. I've seen better roads through bombed-out rice paddies. Right in the middle, like the bumpy spine of an old plow horse, lie the hills. Settlers, half-civilized or not, gave it back to the state. A cornstalk would need hands to stay on these side hills. It was the Sunday circuit for road hunters until the south side finally gave in to the rocks underneath. Township road money had better purposes than maintaining a narrow two-rut track from the abandoned Pedersen farm on one corner to the neighboring Hoefs' farm on the other. A sign was erected at each end proclaiming that it was a low-maintenance road and any travel past that point was "at your own risk." Which I felt was an exaggeration, since the victim was often a vehicle's oil pan and almost never the driver himself.

Being a foot hunter, I regard the condition of the road as irrelevant. I parked my old car on the Hoefs' farm pasture and walked east to enter the Wood Row Creek covers at their junction with the Pedersen farm. This corner is the Bridge covert I wrote about in an earlier chapter; it was and remains a formidable challenge to man, dog, and dry feet.

The guide to the Maple Hills met me by the side of the road one bright sunny afternoon. I don't road hunt. As a result, my speed was picking up so that I could climb the steep road without downshifting. I had just crossed the sand hole at the bottom of the grade when I saw the unmistakable brown triangle of a grouse standing motionless on the side of the road. I stopped, let the cloud of dust pass over the car, and looked in my rearview mirror. He stood quite still, aloof, imperious, as if to say: "See here, come back to this spot; I have some business to discuss with you."

I am not such a purist that I will pass up an opportunity; I just don't look for them on a regular basis. I backed up, as bidden. When I was close enough for conversation, he stepped off the road and into the bush. I killed the motor, stepped out on the gravel, and walked to the back of the car. I had the little brown American water spaniel at that time. She was a fine road hunter. In fact, she cultivated all vices to a fine edge. When the hatch came up, she burst out, hit the road and charged into the underbrush, raising a five- or six-bird covey and scattering them back into the woods. I didn't even have my gun out of its case (as I said, I am a poor road hunter).

But I can take a hint. I drew the shotgun out of its holster, slipped into my vest, and followed the birds. A grouse seldom flies fifty yards, even less if it's not frightened. Just as it is preparing to land it will bank to the left or right to spoil its air speed, and settle down. Then it will trot a few feet and squat down to wait. I picked one of the two or three flight lines, stepped over to the right five or ten yards, and headed into the woods, walking straight and fast about fifty yards. Then I stood still. After two or three minutes I was sure no bird was within ten yards. Remember, I did not have the benefit of a pointing dog to seek out the birds directly or even a good dog that would flush them toward me. The little water spaniel was busy scuffling about in the nearby weeds, but in an unfocused, chipmunk sort of way.

The next trick was to work in three overlapping cloverleafs, one to the left, one to the front, and then one to the right. The first bird was on the left. Walking-up grouse without the aid of a good pointing dog is like searching for booby traps. It is a wired, hands-on-the-gun kind of hunt. The shots are close and fast in a poke-and-pull type of opportunity. My reflexes were fast enough for the bird. I picked it up, put it in my game bag, and made a front loop, stopping halfway through the circle to look at a long narrow opening in the brush.

Old trails are easier to see in the fall. The weeds and grass are different from the tall brush and leaves. The ruts may be grassed in, but the hazel bushes on each side bend over the road bed rather than grow up in it. Oftentimes the deer make use of the passageway, nibbling the wood along the sides. It is not an obvious difference, but in the disorder of the forest the appearance is clearly manmade.

This trail was old; it ran on the flat ground parallel to the big hill. Trails like this make my stomach tight. It might end around the corner or go up the side of a tree into a squirrel hole. Or it just might be the main line to a world of new

grouse covers. The new ones are usually timber-hauling roads—
not very interesting. The old ones are addictive. A skillful
geologist can follow a rock formation for miles just by looking
for similar elements sticking above the ground. The same
principle applies to old-trail sleuthing. Sometimes the clue
is on the ground in the shape of the undergrowth. The line
of an old road can be seen even in the heaviest growth by
getting down and sighting along the path. A triangular tunnel gives it away. If the trail seems to end, a careful look at
the trees can show several standing in a line. In poor light
it appears like a gray hallway. The satisfaction of curiosity
is only part of the reward. The old trails lead to old home-
steads. These in turn are openings in the forest that act as
magnets for grouse.

I followed its course, lifting the overhanging twigs out
of my way and looking ahead for the faint side walls in the
brush. In a few hundred yards I could make out a bright

fiery red color all across the way. A few more yards showed me an opening covered with sumac, and next to it a water-filled pothole. I had not flushed any more grouse, setting aside my bird-finding instincts in searching for the trail origins. Now that I had found the old homestead, I returned to my original purpose, flushing grouse. The water spaniel was elsewhere. I continued along the little lake, turning to pass between two small hills. The woods had opened up into an oak grove and the little path disappeared under the accumulated leaves.

Climbing the smaller of the two little hills, I startled a grouse that flew through the open trees. The sight of it, wide open and obvious, mesmerized me. By the time I remembered to mount the gun it was out of range. But I could see it sit down on a patch of foliage next to a black stump, where it strutted about like a small turkey.

"Why, you puffed up little prince, just stay there for a moment," I said, and promised to be right over.

I watched him intently until I saw the patch of foliage move. It became a deer that had been there all the time, watching me move around. The grouse had tipped the deer's hand. The buck was not in a hurry; he owned these woods. Water could have pooled on his back. I had never seen a deer that big, except perhaps on magazine covers. He crossed the hilltop and disappeared. I turned my gaze back to the grouse, but he was gone.

I circled the pond looking for the grouse, but mostly looking for the next segment of the trail. A second walk through the sumac clearing yielded no more than my first trip until I saw the dark green top of a tall pine beyond the two little hills. It was a custom in the early timbering years to leave a pine standing at a trail intersection in the fashion of a road sign. There was no apparent evidence on the ground nearby, but a push through the hazel brush between the clearing and the old pine brought me to its base, where I found the intersection. A V-shaped cut was still apparent in the earth. The tip of the V pointed toward my little clearing and each leg fanned out into ancient road ruts. The right-hand path led towards the two hills. I had already been there. So I took the left.

As I wrote earlier, a man can't get lost if he doesn't care where he's going. With a road on each side I figured the worst trouble I could get into would only put me a half-mile from "found."

If my path was the original road through this country it would take me to another clearing or a fenceline. That is the problem with exploring. It takes your mind off what's really important. My shotgun was dangling in my fingers when a grouse flushed. It was one of those times when even lifting the gun is useless.

The flush reminded me that I had come a long way, with no return other than increasing my knowledge of the local geography. Consequently, when I stepped into the next opening I was already thinking about how to get back.

This place had the remnants of an old cabin. The builder had been of Scandinavian descent—probably Finnish, because the log corners were cut in the Finns' dovetail fashion. I sat on the wall and packed my pipe, pushing the tobacco in while thinking of the shortest route back to the car.

Straight across country was my conclusion. There would be no birds, and it would be heavy going, but I would be able to save some time and use it to hunt the Wood Row Creek side of the hills.

I was right about the heavy going. By the time I cut the county road my face was wet with sweat, my shirt unbuttoned, and I would have lapped puddle water. The sun was almost set, and there was not enough time to go to another spot.

My little brown water spaniel heard me coming. She was well rested from her afternoon nap under the car, bouncing around under my feet, ready to go. I ignored her and, with the weary footfalls of a tired bird hunter, walked toward my car.

I looked up the road. The sight of the old Kamikaze was as welcome as the water jug inside. There was one thing more on the road between the car and me. A brown triangular shape. Standing still, imperious, and aloof, was the guide grouse. The troublemaker that had got me into this thing. I wanted to shoot him more at that moment than I wanted a drink of water. And I wanted a drink of water more than I wanted life itself.

The brown water spaniel saw him too. The road was dry, and each time that dog put its paws down a spurt of dust rose under its feet. I used the last little bit of energy to sprint after it, trying to close the distance between the grouse and myself.

The bird stood his ground. Wellington at Waterloo could not have been firmer. The water spaniel started to hit the brakes when it saw that the bird was not going to move. I did the same until, finally, at the last moment, the grouse flew up, dusting a shaft of sunlight in the air.

I was ready. I threw down on it with my fast, lightweight Model 31 and slapped the trigger. It went "click."

I had covered miles of brush, weeds, and hard walking with an empty gun!

The grouse was climbing into the open air above the road. It was a rare moment. I bowed to it by making that small scraping noise in the back of my throat. You know, the sound we always make when something really stupid has just happened and it's all our fault.

I still had one thing going for me. It was a pumpgun. I shucked the action and tried again. The gun went off, and the grouse, still unperturbed, dropped back to the road, feet down, head up, where it regained its feet.

The spaniel jumped in to grab it. The grouse rose up about a foot and pounced on the spaniel's head! Both jumped back to eye one another. The dog circled warily and the bird crouched, tail high, head down and hissing.

They had raised a cloud of road dust and this floated in the air around them, yellow in the sun. I had forgotten to load the gun; I forgot I had one.

The spaniel tried again, striking low, but the grouse pecked the dog's head and struck with its wings, rolling the dog over. The grouse stood firm, and the brown water spaniel backed off to do the only thing left to be done. It barked.

I applauded, I cheered, and I laughed. My noisy-crowd antics reminded the bird that there were bigger problems than the spaniel and it flew off—in, I might add, no real hurry.

Climbing the hill is a hard pull, for this road was built before heavy equipment. Sometimes the old car would slide to one side or the other trying to gain a bite on the stones. Once the top was crossed the other side went down at a lesser grade until the bottom, where there used to be a pothole. Not a hole in the road—a water-filled pond. At this point the road circled the pond and it made a lovely entrance to the next quarter-mile because just as the car straightened out, an archway lay before it.

Whenever I came to this part I thought of long roads in pictures of Europe. The kind with a row of Lombardy poplar on each side. The sort of textured landscape that impressionist painters liked to create: A long straight line to set off shadows and bushy leaftops. The difference made this place even better; the trees here were maples. Huge old trees as big around as my arms, with tops and limbs that interlocked over the road. When the fall drained out the leaves, red and yellow filled the sky all the way to the corner. On each side the ripe grain set off the straight dark trunks—it was a living masterpiece...until progress replaced the landscape with modern art.

In the minimalist fashion, the trees were removed. They had shaded the road, and in the spring this section had been slow to dry out. The shoulder of the road got soft next to the pothole. Therefore the only thing to do was to cut the trees and straighten the right-of-way. I wish the neighbors had been a little more unsettled, or perhaps it was the low-slung parts on new cars that dragged in the ruts. Whatever the reason, some of that in-bed-before-nine infected the rough edges of the Maple Hills, and tamed the road.

The hills are lovely as ever. But even the stem on a rose has thorns. We need some rough roads. The kind with bushy edges and small round pieces of gravel. Grouse need grit for their crops, and little boys need a chance to shoot their first grouse on a late afternoon. As I had done, about a hundred feet from where those big old maples used to be.

Chapter 20

Packing for the Trip

Heaven is generally accepted as a place that is out there somewhere among the stars. Which keeps it all neat and clean. We, on the other hand, are here muddling through the muck as best we can. I suppose that gives us something to look forward to, kind of like those clean, comfortable rooms the motel advertising voice talks about on the radio. But if eternity is the length we suppose it to be, such a concept of heaven would give me a bit too much time to watch cable TV and make a few of those free local calls. And if the elevation is what they say it is, chances are the room is a bit too cool for comfort as well.

I have lunch at the Pine Wood cafe every noon. I don't have to order. I just walk in the door, go to the last, or second to the last, stool at the counter, and sit down. My coffee appears, followed by a saucer with two peanut butter cookies, and a sandwich made of the daily special between two slices of wheat bread. Sometimes I walk behind the counter and pick up the daily paper; other times one of the waitresses slides the pages under my hand.

I read the back columns. The front pages are always filled with what I call Hemingway News. You know: love, war, and the lack of both. Anyway, according to the paper, survivors of near-death experiences have reported intense light penetrating the surrounding darkness. Sounds a lot like stars in the sky. But no wonder: the paper is written in big cities by reporters talking to city people. I like the rest of the story. The author says that other, more rural, scenes have been related. Gardens, forests, castles, golf courses—and yes, even cities with skyscrapers—have been reported. The article suggests that the next world for our departing souls may have as many topographies as this one. Even better, our immortal coil may enter heaven at different locations.

I like that idea and I have embraced it. It is not improbable to suggest that our past experiences might well dictate where we spend eternity. Some lawyers I know are in for a big surprise.

As for me, I spend a lot of time in the woods, building memories. A lot of those experiences are in these pages.

It's not a new idea. In his book *Big Woods*, William Faulkner wrote about this through the character Sam Fathers, an old man, the son of a Negro slave and a Chickasaw chief. Faulkner fashioned him as one who lived as a model of natural wisdom and virtue in harmony with the Big Bottom, a vast wilderness. He set him up as a touchstone to compare against those who bought the land and sold it, and bound others to it as tenants or slaves. Sam is a key figure in the book's most famous story, "The Bear," perhaps the greatest hunting story written. But it is the second story, "The Old People," that contains a scene in which Sam, quietly instructing the boy he would mold into a man true to the wilderness and to himself, recognizes as kin a tremendous buck that appears in the woods and salutes him as "Chief" and "Grandfather."

Later, when the boy relates the story to another man, the man explains:

"The earth don't want to just keep things, hoard them; it wants to use them again. Look at the seeds, the acorns, at what happens even to carrion when you try to bury it: it refuses too, seethes and struggles too until it reaches light and air again, hunting the sun..."

As Loren Eiseley said, we each need to possess a wilderness and consider what marvels are to be observed there. If all we take with us on our long eternity is the content of what we have in our memories, then the earth is where we pack our bags.

Of course, I don't spend all my time in the woods, just the last three months of the year. The rest of the time I spend sorting through people's problems, including a few of my own.

We don't pack life's baggage with every event. We just learn enough to get the job done and move on. Every now and again something happens that makes a difference. It ends up in the bag. Sometimes we pack it; sometimes it jumps in there all by itself.

Take, for instance, all those lunches I have at the counter of the Pine Wood. I can't remember what I had to eat yesterday, let alone who I talked to. But I can tell you in close detail almost every lunch I have eaten in the churchyard of Maple Hill Lutheran Church. Why does that place make a difference?

It is where I have lunch with my daughter Elly. Every covert in my grouse hunting world also happens to be within a few miles of the little white church. It doesn't hurt the beauty of the place that it lies at the foot of the tallest of the Maple Hills. It is easy to find, so I can tell my far-flung hunting partners where to regroup.

The churchyard already had a lot of things going for it before I came to stay. The township road that goes by its front door used to be a pretty fair grouse producer. Back in the days when a bright Sunday morning urged road hunters out early, my dad cruised up to the edge of the big stone corner marker in his black '47 Chevrolet. The churchyard was mowed, of course, but all around it the young regrowth had sprung up. Standing next to the cemented pillar of stones was a grouse, pecking gravel. My brother and I were tight with excitement. As the final chorus of the opening hymn drifted across the yard, the peace was split with the blast of Dad's shotgun. He got the grouse, and a lot of stares as white faces pressed against the windows in startled surprise. I know something now that I didn't know then.

The balsam pines shade the graveyard. They were just saplings then. Right next to the church we used to have a huge balsam. It died this year. I counted the rings on the stump. It was 155 years old. My daughter was eleven months.

The oldest pines in the churchyard are now fifty years old. The oldest grave I have ever seen is just over the hill on the Pedersen farm. It belongs to Laura. I have had lunch with her a few times, and I talked to her once.

The weather had warmed up after a cold beginning. I had stood in the churchyard a couple weeks earlier as dry wisps of snow blew across the frozen ground and eddied around the little mound of new-thrown earth. If it is true that the dark matter of this universe flows through us and all things like air through living screens, then it must have been free to pass through a hole as big as the one in my soul. One of my own was lying under the boughs of the balsam pines.

She was alive and smiling, sharing my early morning oatmeal as I prepared to go out deer hunting. How could such a sturdy bundle of life evaporate like that? There was no way to know that she would never again sit on my left leg, inside the warm circle of my arms, and gurgle happily with every other spoonful. She died in her mother's arms, held tightly but not tightly enough to hold back the little spirit that slipped away.

While the ambulance sped at full siren I walked in the crunching snow, following an old deer track, thinking about hot coffee.

I had to do something. A couple times I tried to take a short trip, but every time I got a few miles from home I had to turn around and come back. I was afraid something else might happen. I was standing guard, believing that my presence could somehow protect my family. I didn't want to think about how my life had been changed, irrevocably, in the flash of an instant.

I decided to go grouse hunting. It was a November thaw, close after Thanksgiving. I ended up at Laura Pedersen's grave, way back in the woods. I sat on the stone and talked my way through what had happened and how I felt about it. Of course I had the same conversation with my wife, but this time I could say what I wanted without fear of adding to her burden. Afterwards, I felt better and walked back to the car, following the old trail, over the creek and past the house ruins. Then I turned into the Disco covert and hunted along the road until I came to the big grassy field, sitting golden and frosty in the sun. I crossed the width of it until I came up against the wood's edge and stood there with the sun on my back.

My dogs were puzzled by the pace of this hunt and the mood. They had decided to simply walk along with me. My old Lab Dixie stood very close, slapping my leg with her tail and looking up. Salty the setter made small casts into the sides of the trail. She entered the woods close by the field and slipped gracefully through the hazel-brush clumps. The corner where the field met the trail was a favorite haunt of the birds that lived in this covey.

I couldn't have been less prepared. Salty passed a sunlit bundle of weeds and brush and suddenly spun to her left in a half-circle. She was sight-pointing a grouse. Just as quickly, the grouse flushed off the ground and flew toward me, staying inside the trees but traveling along the field. I moved in the same manner as she had moved. I simply reacted to what I saw. The gun fired, the bird tumbled, and Dixie made a quick retrieve.

When things go bad, they are supposed to stay bad. This did not fit. I was afraid to feel good. I was willing to feel good, but not until next year some time. What would people say?

"Three weeks after his daughter dies and he is out shooting partridge, what a horse's patoot!"

The undeniable truth, however, was soft and beautiful in my hands, and I felt better! I quit then—being a good Norwegian I didn't want to get too much of a good thing— and walked back to the car. I started the motor and drove out the lane onto the township road and ended up at the church. I took out my sandwich and coffee and sat down in front of her headstone.

I looked around and seeing no one else, I explained what had happened. The dogs had Elly's share of my lunch, every other bite. When I put the thermos back behind the car seat my eyes fell on the long and lovely fan of colors in the bird's tail. Reaching in, I plucked two of the feathers and returned to her headstone. I bent down on my knees and placed them, just so, one crossing over the other, under the edge of the red granite.

I have done the same every year since her death. You could see them there today, and yet, by fall they will be gone so that I can do it again.

I think Elly likes all the company. The setters and Brittanies running across her ground, lapping up their food and water, are a canine match for their masters doing the same with sandwiches and coffee. A midday nap to spread the day's heat until it cools in the late afternoon. This year tall, lanky Andy Vance pitched stones across the road to hit an imaginary strike zone on a ditch maple while Elly's brother, Max, pulled weeds from her green cover.

Most of the time it is just the two of us. After my nap I can stretch like a sun-warmed old cat and gaze out across the next field. Over there, by the far fence, Elly's sister Tessa, my oldest child and first hunter, killed her first grouse on the wing. She was walking next to me but out a ways in the scattered clumps of pasture trees and weeds. I was next to the fence watching old Salty work between us until a grouse flushed from Tessa's far side. It crossed us in full speed, stretching its neck and driving its short, powerful wings to reach the trees. As I swung my shotgun up to follow, it exploded in a puff of feathers, centered by a superb shot. My daughter had made the impossible possible.

I can't see it from the churchyard, but I know right where a young Luke Habein stepped over a log and onto the back of a hidden deer. Their separate, and panicked, reactions adding spice to an already memorable story. Not very far from there his dad, my hunting partner Bill, cornered a covey of grouse inside an old hunting cabin and retold the story many times of one bird flying through the roof hole and the other through the open door. You've heard of grouse flying back toward the hunter? In a covert about a mile over the top of that hill I saw Bill shoot an incoming grouse out of the air and catch it like a punted football.

I have walked the bottom of Wood Row Creek from its slow oozing start out of the big swamp to its culvert under the road. The mallards have landed in its beaver ponds so close to my blind that the mist from their wings blew into my face. I have walked the shining edge of those beaver dams where the water meets the sticks and mud. Sometimes I have slipped into the water; sometimes I have made it across to the far shore and the grouse coverts there.

If I could climb to the top of the church steeple I could see all my coverts and all these memories of life on this earth. So many things within these few miles have touched my heart, and none of it had anything to do with my guile, persuasion, implements, or ambitions. I like to think that if indeed I am a living sponge for the dark matter of cosmic wind to blow through, I have perhaps exchanged a few of my molecules for those of the grass and weeds. Maybe a flushing grouse left behind an invisible vapor trail that drifted through me. Why not? My dog seems to smell it. Far better this than the exhaust of a yellow taxi.

I have traded my time for memories. Some are wrapped carefully in tissue to preserve them through the long journey, and others are stains on the bag. Some I wanted and others I couldn't avoid. The best of these have been with other humans or in natural places. The worst as well. For I have been loved by wonderful people and shot at by others. In the natural places nature also has two sides.

A pair of well-dressed nuthatches cleared the debris from a squirrel hole in a box elder outside my office window. They moved in to raise a family. I watched them with joy and pride, looking forward to the day when the fat little ones would tumble out to meet the world. I am often gone to court. The starling could have waited for any of those days. I watched it land on the branch next to the little burrow. I stood up as it entered the nest hole. I shouted at it as the murdering bird held each struggling chick in its yellow beak, killed it, and dropped it to the green grass below. I traded that many minutes of my life for a stain.

But I watched it and it was real. No television screen played it back to me. No politician tried to pass a law against it. No animal rights activist declared the starling cruel and heartless and went off to raise money to protect the offspring of nuthatches.

I will spend my life seeking to make those memories that will outlast it. I will add elements to my life experience until they put me in the ground right next to my little daughter, under the limbs of the balsam pine in the Maple Hill Lutheran churchyard. When they do, I hope to have put together enough good times to enter heaven at a place just like this one.